SHIPWRECKS

AROUND

WALES

Volume One

*COVER PICTURE. Wreck of the NORMAN COURT off
Rhosneigr in 1883 from a painting by Brian Entwistle.
A limited edition of numbered and signed prints are
available from the artist at Noddfa, Station Road,
Rhosneigr, Ynys Môn, Gwynedd.*

SHIPWRECKS

AROUND

WALES

Volume One

Tom Bennett

Published by Happy Fish, Newport, Dyfed, Wales. SA42 OLX.

By the same Author;

Welsh Shipwrecks, Volume One, Aberdyfi to St. David's Head. (1981).
Welsh Shipwrecks, Volume Two, St. David's Head, Pembrokeshire Islands to St. Ann's Head. (1982).
Welsh Shipwrecks, Volume Three, Milford Haven, St. Govan's Head, Tenby and Carmarthen Bay. (1983).
Fishguard Lifeboats. (In aid of RNLI funds, 1984).

Printed and bound in Wales.
Typesetting by Budget Typesetting set in 11 on 12 Times.
Page Layout by Gill Tyas.
Printed by D. Brown & Sons Ltd., Cowbridge and Bridgend.

British Library Cataloguing in Publication Data

Bennett, Tom, 1947 -
    Shipwrecks around Wales.
    Vol. 1
    1. Shipwrecks – Wales – History
    I. Title
    363.1'23'09429 DA731.2

ISBN 0 9512114 0 4

Contents

Photographs & Illustrations

Author, 13,15,16,18,19,20,22,23,25,26,30,32,33,34,38,39,43,46,48,
        55,56,58,59,60,61,62,66,74,75,78,79,80,81,82,84,85,89,92,
        93,94,97,102. Photographer unknown,17,42,45,53,
Mr B.Andrews, 40
Mr K.Bates, 84
Mr B.Burgess,21
Mr T.Bowen, 51
Mr P.Concannon, 31
Mr D.Davies, 51,52
Mr B.R.Entwistle, Cover picture
Mr J.Evans, 95
Henry Parry Collection, Gwynedd Archives Service, 29,41,83,98
Sir J.Houlder, 67
Mr V.Morris, 82
Norsk Sjofartsmuseum, Oslo, 35
Mr T.Owens, 37
Mr R.M.Parsons, 24
Mr J.Phillips, 64,65,72
Richard Larn Collection, 57,88
Royal National Lifeboat Institution, 54
MOD (Navy), 73
Studio Jon Ltd., 47
The Illustrated London News, 10,11,69,90,91,92,100,101,103
Mr A.Wareing, 27
Mr & Mrs Williams, 70
Mrs V.A.Wisbey, 71
World Photos, 77

The author wishes to thank everyone for their co-operation in
providing photographs.

Because of the transient nature of shipwrecks and the fact that they often occur at night or
in atrocious weather conditions, photographic records of the event are rare. The author
would like to hear from anyone who has photographs or postcards of shipwrecks lost on the
coast of Wales or would appeal for them to be taken to the nearest County Records Office
so that these historic pictures are not lost to future generations.

Introduction

For thousands of years seafarers have sailed along the shores of Wales. To reach the port of Liverpool, mariners have had to round the North Wales coast and the treacherous Skerries rocks, and to reach Bristol have had to contend with the Bristol Channel with its gales, shifting sand-banks and strong currents.

Throughout the nineteenth century the South Wales ports were some of the busiest in the world, exporting vast quantities of coal. Ships and the sea have been an integral part of the communities of Wales and the coastal towns not only built fine trading ships but also produced some of the most renowned and beloved sea captains.

This book is a collection of over fifty true stories of men who have suffered at sea, of men, who have successfully rescued others, and of vessels of all shapes, sizes and nationalities which have been lost around the coast of Wales.

Acknowledgements

I would like to thank all who have helped with this book. To my wife Maureen, for her patience in correcting the text and to diving pals past and present, especially Roger Strawbridge, Bruce Jones, Dave Moore, Greg Evans, Jim Phillips and to Clive Hayes of the City Garage at St. David's.

To all those who have kindly let me copy photographs; Bryan Andrews of 'Kelpies', T.W. Belt, Barrie Burgess, Donald Davies, B. R. Entwistle, John Evans, Gwynedd Archive Service, John Houlder, G. James, RNLI, Roscoe Howells, Richard Larn, Dr. George Middleton, R. M. Parsons, Jim Phillips, Studio Jon and Mrs. V.A. Wisbey.

My appreciation is also extended to the staff at the National Maritime Museum, Greenwich; The Welsh Industrial and Maritime Museum, Cardiff; and the National Maritime Museum, Oslo; the librarians at the National Libraries of Wales and Scotland; and those at Haverfordwest Library and at the Pembrokeshire Records Office.

Every endeavour has been made to eliminate errors. If mistakes are found, I apologize and would hope that readers will let me know so that they can be rectified for future editions.

Tom Bennett
February 1987
Pembrokeshire

Causative Factors of Shipwrecks Around Wales

The introductory remarks of the Sailing Directions for the Bristol Channel dated 1868 commences; ' Mariners navigating the Bristol and St George's Channels, should always pay the greatest attention to the velocity and direction of the tides; for there is commonly a northerly indraught, which, setting obliquely towards the shores of Wales, particularly between Hartland Point and Holyhead, frequently drives a vessel out of her regular course, and occasions most fatal accidents. The direction and force of the current will materially depend on the wind and tide; and the mariner navigating from the Land's End towards Dublin, will find himself insensibly carried to the eastward....vessels, therefore, when off the western coast of Wales, particularly in dark and foggy weather, and with westerly winds, cannot be too careful in shaping their respective courses; for should they neglect such precaution, they will incur the danger of being wrecked'.

This is just one of a whole host of factors which can contribute to a ship being lost around the coast of Wales. The Board of Trade categorized shipping casualties in the latter nineteenth century into the following headings;

Stranding ie, hitting the coast or breaking up on a sandbank.
Collision ie, hitting another vessel.
Fire ie catching fire.
Foundered ie, sinking at sea (the word is founder not flounder!).
Abandoned ie, left by the crew, vessel probably sank soon after.
Condemned ie, declared unfit, often broken up ashore.
Unknown Fate ie, missing vessel.

About half of all shipwrecks were due to stranding, and subsequently breaking up. About 12% foundered, this figure being about the same for both sailing vessels and steamers. The following details for March 1891 show causative factors split between sailing vessels and steamers, it shows some interesting differences;

SAILING VESSELS
56% lost due to Stranding.
5% Lost due to Collision.
2% Lost due to Fire.
10% Lost due to Foundering.
14% Lost due to Abandoned.
8% Lost due to Condemned.
5% Lost, Unknown Fate.

STEAMERS
44% Lost due to Stranding.
36% Lost due to Collision.
13% Lost due to Foundering.
7% Lost, Unknown Fate.

As can be seen 1 in 3 steamers was lost by collision yet this cause was only responsible for 1 in 20 sailing vessel losses.

From the statistics we also know that sailing ship losses reached a peak in 1864 and then steadily declined whereas there was still an increase in steamer losses until 1880 and then they also declined. Steam engines became more efficient and reliable and larger ships manned by fewer crewmen gradually came onto the scene in the period from 1880 to 1910. This has progressed into modern times when just a handful of tankers and cross channel ferries can accommodate the same cargo tonnages as a vast fleet of trading schooners.

It is too easy to dismiss the reasons for bygone shipwrecks as being the result of inadequate navigation, bad seamanship or insufficiently equipped vessels. Undoubtedly these have caused some of the tragedies but it must be remembered that just over one hundred years ago when most shipwrecks were occuring there were enormous numbers of ships sailing around the coast of Wales.

In one year (1855) there were 5,369 ships,(414,686 tons) entering the five major ports of Cardigan Bay. For the same year it was estimated that the annual tonnage up and down St George's Channel was at least 11,000,000.

In 1879 it was calculated that for British vessels inwards and outwards, to and from UK ports in one year averaged 600,000 representing a tonnage of 102,000,000 and having between three and four million people on board. A comment was made at that time by the Pembrokeshire Herald of the 'fewness' of serious and fatal shipping disasters when compared with these shipping numbers.

With these wrecks was a tragic loss of life; in the eight years between 1851 and 1858 there were 5,020 lives lost and 7,441 ships wrecked around the coast of Britain. In the twenty-five years from 1855 to 1879 there were 49,322 shipwrecks in the UK recorded by the Board of Trade. The loss of life from these amounted to 18,319 lives.

The British Isles has by far the greatest number of shipwrecks per mile of coastline than anywhere else. Richard Larn, author of many shipwreck books, has said that there are at least 250,000 shipwrecks around Britain. The British Sub Aqua Club have said 500,000, a figure I think of as being rather high, but does anybody know ? After all there are thousands of vessels that have been lost without trace, unrecorded in the pages of history.
For instance in one month in June 1874 the following figures are given. Throughout the world there were 115 sailing vessels lost (58 British), 11 steamers lost (4 British) and over 17 other vessels reported as missing. This, remember, in a summer month which for Wales would have had the least number of wrecks. Shipping registers held in HM Customs Houses around the coast frequently show a final entry of 'Missing', where the vessel and her entire crew have vanished. One typical entry of the 68 ton New Quay, Cardigan schooner LOUISA JANE, built at Appledore in 1859 merely states 'Disappeared 1873 after leaving Milford'.

At the end of the nineteenth century about 1 out of every 8 shipwrecks in the UK was around the Welsh coast.

Throughout the latter half of the last century the Board of Trade kept records of United Kingdom ship losses. Some representative totals are given below;

Year 1855 - 1,141 wrecks
Year 1859 - 1,416
Year 1863 - 1,664
Year 1868 - 2,131
Year 1871 - 1,575
Year 1875 - 3,757
Year 1878 - 3,002
Year 1880 - 1,303
Year 1909 -   733

These were the figures despite the tremendous rescues carried out by individuals and thousands of lives saved by the Lifeboat crews. The RNLI which was formed in 1824 was responsible for the planning and strategy of establishing and funding numerous Lifeboat stations around the coast. By 1868 there were 29 Lifeboats in Wales, 162 in England, 31 in Scotland and 28 in Ireland. The RNLI still performs this valuable service and we must remember that it does so without Government funds and relies entirely on our voluntary donations.

Lifeboatmen, too, have been lost around the Welsh coast while attempting rescues; 5 were lost from the Rhoscolyn Lifeboat in 1927, 7 from the Rhyl crew in 1852, 13 from Point of Ayr in 1857, the entire Mumbles crew of 8 in 1947 and 4 Mumbles Lifeboatmen were lost in 1883, 3 Lifeboatmen from St David's in 1910, 3 from the Porteynon Lifeboat in 1916 and there have been many others.

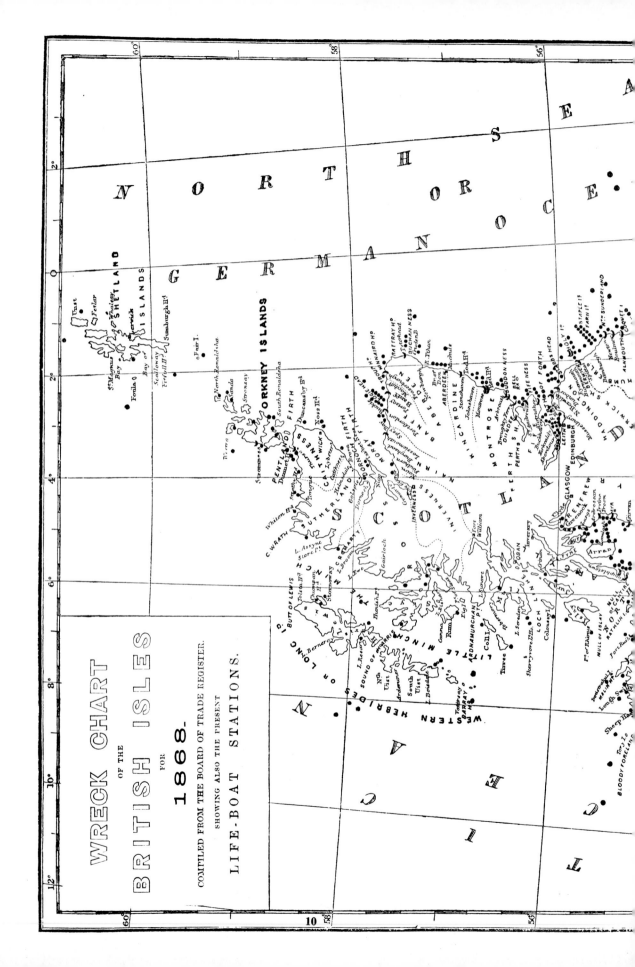

WRECK CHART
OF THE
BRITISH ISLES
FOR
1868.
COMPILED FROM THE BOARD OF TRADE REGISTER.
SHOWING ALSO THE PRESENT
LIFE-BOAT STATIONS.

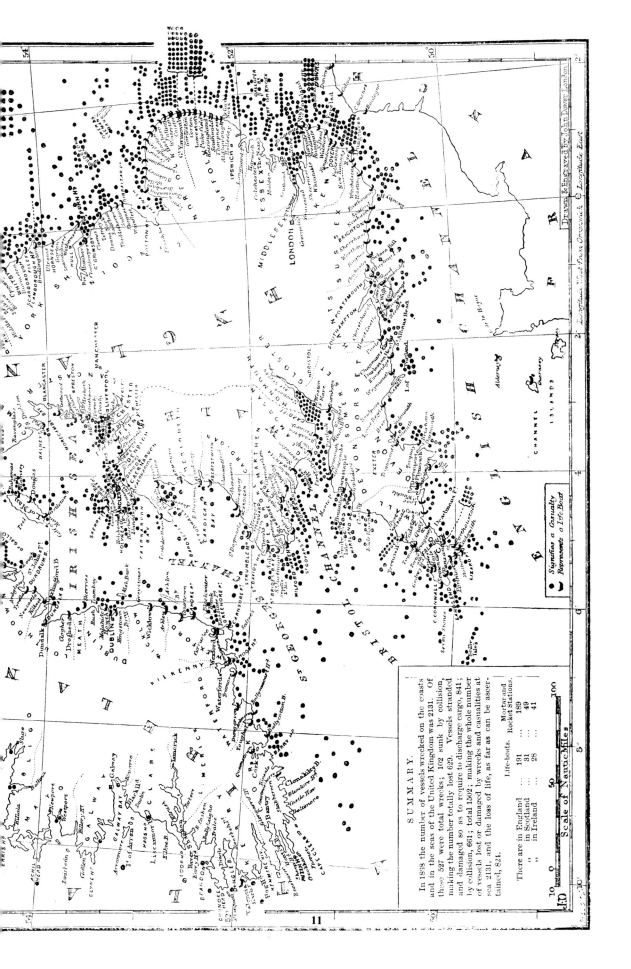

SUMMARY.

In 1858 the number of vessels wrecked on the coasts and in the seas of the United Kingdom was 2131. Of those 527 were total wrecks; 102 sunk by collision, making the number totally lost 629. Vessels stranded and damaged so as to require to discharge cargo, 841; by collision, 661; total 1502; making the whole number of vessels lost or damaged by wrecks and casualities at sea 2131, and the loss of life, as far as can be ascertained, 821.

	Life-boats.	Mortar and Rocket Stations.
There are in England	191	189
,, in Scotland	31	49
,, in Ireland	28	41

● Signifies a Casualty

■ Represents a life Boat

Scale of Nautic Miles

10   0   50   100

Drawn & Engraved by John Dower London.

11

SHIPWRECKS INCLUDED IN THIS BOOK

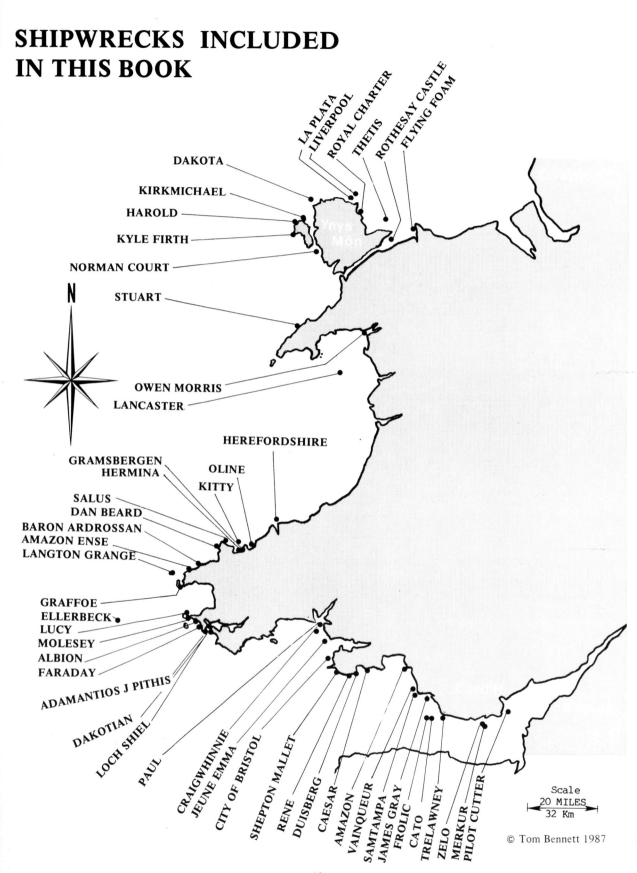

LA PLATA
LIVERPOOL
ROYAL CHARTER
THETIS
ROTHESAY CASTLE
FLYING FOAM

DAKOTA
KIRKMICHAEL
HAROLD
KYLE FIRTH
NORMAN COURT
STUART

Ynys Môn

OWEN MORRIS
LANCASTER

HEREFORDSHIRE

GRAMSBERGEN
HERMINA
OLINE
KITTY

SALUS
DAN BEARD
BARON ARDROSSAN
AMAZON ENSE
LANGTON GRANGE

GRAFFOE
ELLERBECK
LUCY
MOLESEY
ALBION
FARADAY

ADAMANTIOS J PITHIS

DAKOTIAN
LOCH SHIEL
PAUL
CRAIGWHINNIE
JEUNE EMMA
CITY OF BRISTOL
SHEPTON MALLET
RENE
DUISBERG
CAESAR
AMAZON
VAINQUEUR
SAMTAMPA
JAMES GRAY
FROLIC
CATO
TRELAWNEY
ZELO
MERKUR
PILOT CUTTER

Scale
20 MILES
32 Km

© Tom Bennett 1987

12

ADAMANTIOS J PITHIS

Type: Cargo Steamship
Port of Registry: Greece
Official Number: 118239
Tonnage: 4,537 tons gross
Built: 1908, Glasgow
Length: 385 feet
Breadth: 51 feet
Engines: 320 nhp
Date of Sinking: January 27th 1940
Location: St Ann's Head, Milford Haven,
Dyfed

One of the first casualties in the Milford Haven Waterway during World War 11 was not a casualty of war but a loss due to human error. The large Greek steamer ADAMANTIOS J PITHIS was entering the Haven when her Captain made an error of navigation in the January fog.

Lighthousemen living in the cottages at St Ann's Head were astonished to wake up one morning and see a large steamer stranded under the nearby cliffs. They hurried to the spot and were puzzled when they found nobody aboard, the ship was deserted save for two beautiful cats and a fine canary. The men were later to learn that the Captain and 27 members of the crew had been taken off during the night. The Angle Lifeboat had gone to her aid but a naval patrol boat had already taken off Captain Glykas and the whole of the crew.

The ship had a cargo of grain from the Argentinian port of Rosario. The following day the high tide and heavy seas washed over the wreck from bow to stern and she started to break up.

This incident highlighted the vulnerability of large ships entering the mouth of the Haven. Great care has since been taken by the Milford Haven Conservancy Board, the Pilots and the Coastguard to prevent a reoccurrance.

The ship was originally built for the Hogarth Shipping Company in 1908 by Napier & Miller Ltd of Glasgow. Her engines were also built in Glasgow and the ship was named BARON MINTO, the first of three ships to bear this name.
She remained in the Baron Fleet for twenty one years until she was sold to Pithis Bros & Co., and renamed ADAMANTIOS J PITHIS after one of the owners. Since her sinking she has been named 'The Greek' by divers who find her proper name something of a mouthful.

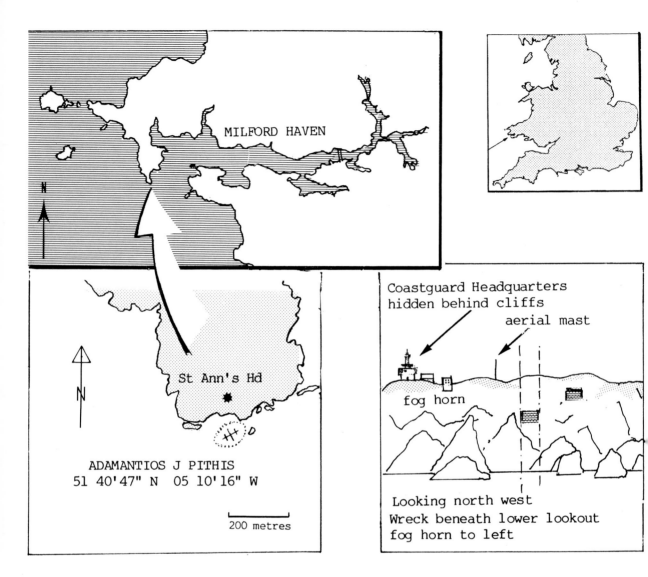

MILFORD HAVEN

St Ann's Hd

ADAMANTIOS J PITHIS
51 40'47" N   05 10'16" W

200 metres

Coastguard Headquarters
hidden behind cliffs

aerial mast

fog horn

Looking north west
Wreck beneath lower lookout
fog horn to left

DIVE DETAILS
Location: 51°40'47" N 05°10'16" W
Depth: 10m to 16m
Seabed: rock & small boulders
Currents: strong at times, keep in
Underwater Visibility: fair
Launch Site: Dale

ALBION

Type: Paddle Steamer
Port of Registry: Bristol
Tonnage: 270 tons (old measurement)
Built: 1831
Length: 150 feet
Date of Sinking: April 19th 1837
Location: Albion Beach, Marloes,
　　　　　　Pembrokeshire, Dyfed

The ALBION was one of the fastest of the early steamers managed by the Bristol General Steam Packet Company. Built to high standards by the War Office Company in 1831 she regularly ran a service from Cork to Bristol or Dublin to Bristol.

Captain Bailey was at the helm on April 19th 1837 when the ALBION was returning from Dublin with general goods and passengers. It was a route he was well accustomed to and as they neared the cliffs of Skomer Island some of the 21 passengers were getting excited at the breathtaking scenery. Captain Bailey did not consider he was taking any unnecessary chances by taking his paddle steamer through Jack Sound, it enabled him to shorten his route and he had done it many times before, and besides, it provided his passengers with a sightseeing trip of the spectacular cliffs.

The ALBION, running at a surface speed of over eleven knots, was taken out of control in the fast eddying currents of Jack Sound and hit a submerged rock. With his ship leaking badly Captain Bailey had to act quickly. He continued with the current and steered for the nearest beach just north of Gateholm Island. The ship's boiler fires were put out by the incoming water just as she was hitting the beach. The ALBION settled onto the sand, her decks still above water. A Cardigan sloop nearby saw the dilemma and sailed over to help. All 21 passengers of the ALBION crowded onto the sloop together with all their

possessions until it could carry no more. They arrived safely at Milford the next morning.

The crew of the ALBION stayed with the steamer looking after the variety of animals and the valuable cargo. On board were five horses belonging to Lord Antrim and hundreds of pigs. There was also Irish whisky, linen, wheat and Guinness. The horses were allowed to swim ashore the next day and later stabled. The press reported the following week that 'A good part of the cargo has been got out and a lot of the porter (Guinness) has been sold on the spot. Out of about 400 pigs upwards of 200 have been got on shore by the exertions of the people in the neighbourhood.' The paper did not say that most of the missing pigs had been caught by the Marloes folk and were already being salted in every cottage in the village.

The beach was given the name Albion Beach and the paddle wheel shaft can still be seen rising out of the sea where she was wrecked.

Parts of the paddle steamer ALBION can still be seen at low water where she was lost.

AMAZON

Type: Sailing Ship, 4 Masted Barque
Port of Registry: Greenock
Tonnage: 2062 tons
Built: 1886, Glasgow
Length: 287 feet
Breadth: 42 feet
Date of Sinking: September 1st 1908
Location: Margam Sands, Glamorgan

The night of August 31st 1908 was a wild one. The men on the HELWICK LIGHTVESSEL had to be rescued by Lifeboat and the London full-rigged ship VERAJEAN came ashore near Rhoose Point.

In Swansea Bay the winds reached hurricane force and the fine white hull of the four masted barque AMAZON was straining at her anchor cables. She had already started her outward journey to Iquique, Chile, when the worsening weather had made her anchor for the night in the Outer Roads. It was not a wise decision. The AMAZON was fully laden with coal from Port Talbot and the sheer mass of the large iron ship and her heavy cargo was just too much for her anchors. By 6am both anchor cables had parted and she drifted north easterly onto Margam Sands, near to the old Bar of Avon.

A terrible scene of disaster and destruction followed as towering seas smashed over the decks and broke up the ship's lifeboat just as it was being lowered. Rocket apparatus from the shore would not reach the wreck and the Mumbles Lifeboat could not effect a rescue because the seas were too shallow.

A hurricane in 1908 broke up the strong iron hull of the AMAZON on Margam Sands,
three-quarters of her crew lost their lives.

The ship's masts, one by one, toppled in the turmoil, and the crewmen that were clinging to them were washed into the surf.

Many local men waded out from the beach into the waves to help but to rescue more than a few proved impossible. At the final count it was realized that 20 out of the ship's complement of 28 had perished and another seaman died of pneumonia three days later.

The body of the Captain, Andrew Garrick of Penarth, was discovered eight days later near Sker Point. The crew had lashed him to the mainmast after he had been accidentally knocked unconscious, and his body was found near to the mast.

The twisted iron hull settled into the Morfa Sands and was eventually broken up on site and removed by Thos.Ward & Co, the shipbreakers of Briton Ferry.

Figurehead of the AMAZON.

AMAZONENSE

Type: Cargo Steamship
Port of Registry: Liverpool
Official Number: 81262
Tonnage: 1,791 tons gross
Built: 1879, Southampton
Length: 287 feet
Breadth: 35 feet
Engines: Compound Steam, 170 nhp
Date of Sinking: April 16th 1881
Location: Near Porthgain, Pembrokeshire,
          Dyfed

The trading steamer AMAZONENSE had a short history, built in Southampton in 1881 she only survived two years before being wrecked when outward bound for Brazil. She belonged to the Red Cross Line, R.Singlehurst & Co., which amalgamated with the Booth Line in 1901.

She commenced her final voyage on Friday, April 15th 1881, leaving Liverpool bound for Le Havre and then on to Lisbon and Para, Brazil. Her master was Captain Hallgate who was confronted with a thick fog in St George's Channel, nevertheless he proceeded south relying entirely on his compass. The first indication that he was not on course was an almighty crash as the steamer hit the headland near St David's Head. So sudden was the shock that one crew member died of fright. He was a storekeeper to the engineering section of the ship, fortunately he was the only casualty.

The hull rapidly filled with water and the ship sank in shallow water, leaving the bow above the waves, the stern underwater, and five metres of water in the holds. The hull was so badly damaged that refloating was out of the question and the wreck was sold by auction, where she lay, a few weeks later.

There was an inquiry at her home port of Liverpool in May 1881 and some criticism was

Ship's wheel boss from the AMAZONENSE.

made of Captain Hallgate who had his certificate suspended for three months.

The court deemed that the AMAZONENSE was travelling at 'too high a rate of speed', in other words, far too fast, considering the foggy conditions. The AMAZONENSE was an iron ship and her compasses had not been corrected for the trip.

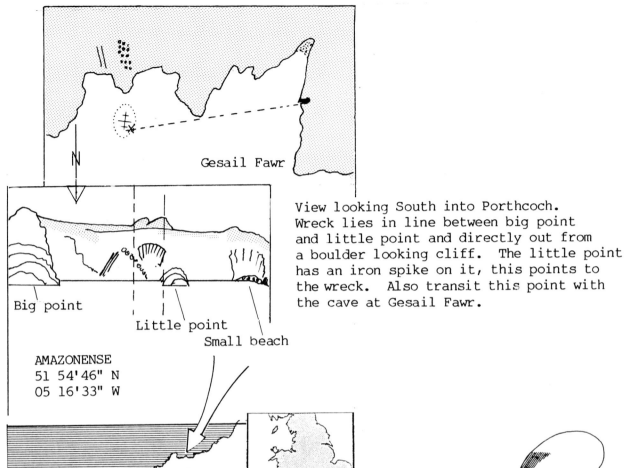

Gesail Fawr

Big point

Little point

Small beach

AMAZONENSE
51 54'46" N
05 16'33" W

ST DAVID'S

View looking South into Porthcoch.
Wreck lies in line between big point
and little point and directly out from
a boulder looking cliff. The little point
has an iron spike on it, this points to
the wreck. Also transit this point with
the cave at Gesail Fawr.

One blade
broken off

BOSS

*Drawing of the broken four-bladed propellor lying at a
depth of 14 metres.*

DIVE DETAILS
Location: 51°54'46" N 05°16'33" W
Depth: 8m to 16m
Seabed: rock, boulders & kelp
Currents: OK close to cliffs
Underwater Visibility: good
Launch Site: Aberieddy or Whitesands

BARON ARDROSSAN (1)

Type: Cargo Steamship
Port of Registry: Ardrossan
Official Number: 79425
Previous Name: EMILE (1891 to 1898)
Tonnage: 1,451 tons gross
Built: 1881, Whitby
Length: 243 feet
Breadth: 34 feet
Engines: Compound Steam, 168 nhp
Date of Sinking: August 21st 1898
Location: Near Porthgain, Pembrokeshire
Dyfed

The BARON ARDROSSAN has an interesting history. Built for Hugh Hogarth in 1881 she sailed the seas for eighteen years. She was the first ship to have the title 'BARON' as part of her name which then became a tradition with the Hogarth Fleet. All Hugh Hogarth's ships were registered at the port of Ardrossan, the port where his business originally started and where he resided. It was thus fitting that this ship was so named. She was the first of six ships to bear this name.

The BARON ARDROSSAN was with Hogarth's fleet until 1891 when she was sold to J.C.Bonnin of France and renamed EMILE. In 1895 she was sold to T.Weissenburger, but three years later she was bought by the Cardiff firm, P.Rowe & Sons who renamed her BARON ARDROSSAN.

With a cargo of coal she left Glasgow at 3am on August 20th 1898. The ship steamed south for St Malo with a crew of 16 on board with the addition of the Captain's wife, their young daughter and a grandson of the owners.
All went well until midnight when they ran into a thick fog. So dense was the fog that it was impossible for Captain Cove to see more than the bows of his ship from the bridge. Wisely he gave the order to slow speed ahead. Already he was on a wrong heading and instead of clearing the Welsh coast he ran his ship onto the rocks near Porthgain.

His wife and daughter were asleep at the time and even the grounding of the steamer did not awake them. When the ship started to settle they were immediately roused from their bunks and, together with the owners' grandson, were put into the first ship's lifeboat. The rest of those on board quickly followed and manned the three ship's lifeboats as the hull of the

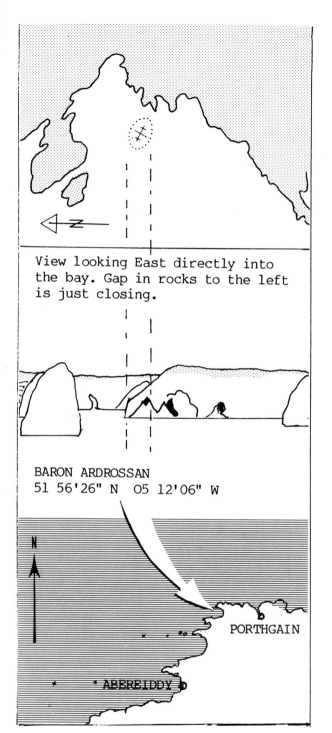

View looking East directly into the bay. Gap in rocks to the left is just closing.

BARON ARDROSSAN
51 56'26" N 05 12'06" W

PORTHGAIN

ABEREIDDY

BARON ARDROSSAN slowly settled beneath the waves. All three boats remained near the wreck for the remainder of the night. At daybreak they could see that the ship had sailed directly into a rocky cove. As the sea was calm and the weather fine they decided to stay in the cove while they put one of the crewmen ashore. He climbed the cliff and went off in search of help, but not knowing the right direction travelled four miles before he came to a cottage. Any other direction and his task would have been much easier. Eventually help arrived and the boats were piloted into the harbour of Porthgain only a mile away.

The bow of the steamer stayed above water for a few days but the stern half of the ship sank so quickly that most of the personal possessions of the crew were lost. The Captain could not retrieve the ship's papers and his wife only managed to gather together a few articles of clothing before she left the ship. Only two of the crew actually recovered their kit and the rest lost all their belongings. With the help of the St David's branch of the Shipwrecked Sailors' Society the crew was sent to their respective homes.

DIVE DETAILS
Location: 51°56'26" N 05°12'06" W
Depth: 9m to 13m
Seabed: rock & sand
Currents: none inside bay
Underwater Visibility: often good
Launch Site: Porthgain or Abereiddy

CAESAR

Type: Admiralty Tender
Port of Registry: British
Tonnage: assume about 60 tons
Date of Sinking: November 29th 1760
Location: Pwlldu Head, Gower, Glamorgan

The CAESAR had a cargo of press ganged men when she drove ashore on the Gower in 1760. The exact numbers of men lost in the incident will remain uncertain but what is known is that no other recorded shipwreck on the Gower has lost so many lives.

The CAESAR was en route from Bristol to Plymouth, in company with another Admiralty tender the REEVES. The Lieutenants aboard had the difficult task of empressing men to the Navy, if offers of bounty did not suffice they would seize and arrest anyone that looked fit enough for the job. After lying at anchor in Mumbles Bay the two sailing vessels made their way to open sea when an adverse tide and deteriorating weather forced their return. Seeing a headland on the port bow the pilot of the CAESAR assumed it to be Mumbles Head and preparations were made to round it and anchor in its shelter. The headland was, in fact, that of Pwlldu and by the time their mistake was realized the vessel was doomed.

With her hull pierced on the rocks the vessel soon began to break apart. The majority of the pressed men were battened down below decks and had little chance of survival with the rising tide. The wreckage washed ashore together with scores of dead bodies.

The Captain of the CAESAR, Adam Drake, and his Lieutenant, survived, together with some of the crew. They escaped by climbing across the bowsprit and up the cliff to High Pennard. Lloyds List (2598, December 2nd)

briefly records the incident with 'The CAESAR Tender, from Bristol for Plymouth, is lost to the westward of the Mumbles, and 62 men and 3 women perished.' A few days later some more bodies had come ashore as the Captain reported that a total of 68 required burial. He was given the task of paying for their burial which was done in a mass grave on the eastern slope of the headland. How many others were lost that night will never be known but some reports say as many as 97 bodies were buried. Only one of the pressed men survived who was cared for by a local man who had successfully resisted an arrest by the same press gang earlier that year.

The cleft in the boulders where the wreck hit is still known as Caesar's Hole and the position nearby where so many were buried is called Gravesend.

CATO (II)

Type: Cargo Steamship
Port of Registry: Bristol
Tonnage: 710 tons gross
Built: 1914, Campbeltown
Length: 230 feet
Breadth: 31 feet
Date of Sinking: March 3rd 1940
Location: Off Nash Point, Glamorgan

Owned by the Bristol Steam Navigation Company, the CATO II was one of the ships most frequently seen passing up the River Avon in the years between the Wars. Her cargo, more often than not, was Guinness from Dublin.

Somehow she had escaped enemy action in World War 1 and when war returned in 1939 she, again, was the only Company ship to be in service. All went well until March 1940 when the CATO was returning from Ireland. She had her usual cargo of Guinness in her holds when a few miles off Nash Point she was struck by a magnetic mine. The ship sank quickly and 13 of her 15 crew were lost.

On sinking some of the cargo freed itself from the hold and a number of barrels of stout washed ashore. The wreck quickly earned the title of the 'Guinness Wreck'. The sight of the barrels delighted the Glamorgan folk living nearby and there are stories of them having communal drinking sessions on the beaches. One barrel was rolled home to a house in Margam, a distance of two miles from where it was discovered, but the most amusing story comes from Pyle. A man from Pyle got a barrel home and poured the brown liquour into the bath. When his wife saw what he had done she was so outraged that she immediately pulled out the plug and he lost the lot!

DIVE DETAILS

Location: 51°23'38" N 03°37'32" W
Depth: 19m to 22m
Seabed: sand & shingle
Currents: strong, 5 knots on springs
Underwater Visibility: nil
Launch Site: Southerndown

SS CATO seen in more peaceful times in the River Avon at her home port of Bristol.

CITY OF BRISTOL

Type: Paddle Steamer, Schooner Rigged
Port of Registry: Bristol
Tonnage: 209 tons
Built: 1827, Bristol
Length: 144 feet
Breadth: 35 feet (including paddles)
Date of Sinking: November 18th 1840
Location: Rhossili Beach, Gower
          Glamorgan

It was a blustery Autumn morning in 1840 when the CITY OF BRISTOL cast off from the quayside at Waterford. The weather was uncertain and after experiencing the wind and swell at Hook Head, Captain Stacy decided to wait awhile. He anchored the paddle steamer in the estuary and as darkness fell and time was pressing on he set course once again for the home port of Bristol. On board were 10 passengers, 17 crew and the usual cargo of farm produce and livestock, which included twenty eight pigs and three cows.

The voyage went well until Caldey Island was sighted over the port quarter. The sky darkened and the wind increased to a strong north westerly blow. Dusk was quickened by the black clouds and visibility dropped rapidly as the storm increased. Captain Stacey was accustomed to finding shelter from storms in the Bristol Channel and knew that he could find an anchorage behind Worm's Head.

In the gloom a headland was sighted and they rounded it believing it was Worm's Head. It

was a fateful mistake for they had rounded
Burry Holmes and were heading directly for the
breakers on Rhossili beach. In horror they
desperately attempted to turn the steamer; but
it was too late. The seas pounded her onto the
sand. The sails were hoisted in an effort to
move her but the hull was only driven further
onto the beach. Huge waves broke over the
deck, terrifying all on board.

Some of the crew and a few passengers were
lost overboard as they tried to launch one of
the boats. Two hours after the steamer had hit
the beach the flooding tide increased the seas,
three heavy breakers struck her one after
another and the ship broke up.

Passengers, crewmen, cattle and barrels were
washed away, many of them never to be seen
again. By morning 25 lives had been lost to the
sea, the only survivors were the ship's
carpenter and one cowman.

News of the disaster spread quickly and by late
morning people had flocked to the beach but
there was not much to be seen. A Swansea
man, who inspected some of the pieces that
had come ashore, commented 'she must have
been a very superior vessel, her timbers are as
sound and substantial as any I have ever seen.'

The CITY OF BRISTOL was built for the
War Office Steam Packet Company in 1827

Parts of the CITY OF BRISTOL still rise above the waves on Rhossili Beach.

and was built to the highest specifications of
the day. She regularly acted as a troopship or
as a conveyance of recruits or convicts to and
from Dublin. From 1836 the Bristol Steam
Navigation Company regularly ran her from
Bristol to Dublin, Cork or Waterford. Parts of
the CITY OF BRISTOL'S twelve foot
diameter paddle wheel mechanism are still
lying amongst the waves at Rhossili and can
easily be seen at low water. Her wreckage
stands as a grave reminder of a simple
navigational error that cost so many lives. For
the wreckage to exist at all after nearly a
century and a half confirms the words of that
Swansea man; she was indeed a very superior
vessel.

CRAIGWHINNIE

Type: Sailing Ship, 3 Masted Barque
Port of Registry: Calcutta
Official Number: 78812
Tonnage: 834 tons register
Built: 1878, Liverpool
Length: 192 feet
Breadth: 33 feet
Date of Sinking: December 20th 1899
Location: Cefn Sidan, Carmarthen Bay
　　　　　　Dyfed

The iron barque CRAIGWHINNIE had been at sea for nearly four months when a heavy gale hit her. The date was December 7th 1899 and she was nearing the end of a long voyage from Calcutta. The gale caused seas to sweep the decks and two boats were smashed and the ship's compass was lost overboard. One of the two steering compasses was damaged leaving only one compass intact which was unreliable. On December 15th an accurate observation was made but for the next five days the weather was foggy and they became stranded in Carmarthen Bay thinking that they were near the Channel Islands. The error in part being due to an inaccurate bearing of Ushant being given to them by another vessel.

The CRAIGWHINNIE stranded on Cefn Sidan at 6am and her signals of distress brought out the Ferryside Lifeboat at 8.50am. Of the 19 men aboard the CRAIGWHINNIE, 17 were taken ashore including the Captain

The iron barque CRAIGWHINNIE, originally of Liverpool, was wrecked on the notorious sand bank of Cefn Sidan at the end of a long voyage from Calcutta.

who wanted to send the unfortunate news to the owners by telegraph. The Chief Officer and the Second Officer remained on board as the sea was calm and everyone was hopeful that she would float off with the next high tide. The CRAIGWHINNIE had a cargo of 1,135 tons of linseed and scrap iron, intended for Hull. The hold was full of hundreds of sacks of linseed, each sack weighing 65 kilos

The ship failed to lift with the high tides and efforts were made to transfer the sacks into smaller local boats.

Tugs were used to try to tow her off, but to no avail. In a desperate struggle to lighten her, local men were employed to cut open the bags and pour the seed overboard, but still the

stranded ship remained. On January 6th the CRAIGWHINNIE'S hull broke in two, and part of her iron bow section can be seen today.

The inquiry reported that her loss was due to careless and negligent navigation, and the Master's certificate was suspended for three months. The Mate was also censured for the careless and unusual way in which the ship's logbook was kept.

One interesting story is remembered. The discarded linseed washed ashore along the banks of the Ferryside estuary, in places it was half a metre deep. Hungry birds soon discovered a welcome source of food and thousands of ducks, geese and finches arrived to spend all winter eating the cargo.

DAKOTA

Type: Liner Steamship
Port of Registry: Liverpool
Tonnage: 4,332 tons gross
Built: 1874, Newcastle Upon Tyne
Length: 401 feet
Breadth: 43 feet
Date of Sinking: May 9th 1877
Location: East Mouse, Amlwch, Ynys Mon

The DAKOTA was a superb liner in her day. She was built by Palmers of Newcastle in 1874 and she was built for speed. The Liverpool and North-Western Steamship Company had their sights on the Blue Riband, but it was not to be. Her original boilers were a disappointment and even the replacement boilers did not produce their designed pressures. Nevertheless the DAKOTA worked on the Atlantic run and it was on one such voyage from Liverpool to New York that she met with disaster.

On the evening of May 9th 1877 the DAKOTA was steaming steadily round the North Wales coast, outward bound. A fresh east south east was blowing but it made little impression on the large liner as she steamed at fourteen knots about two miles off the land.

Amidships, the Fourth Officer stood on the bridge. He took bearings and decided that a course greater than two miles off the coast was more prudent. A change of ship's course was ordered but then an unusual thing happened. Instead of steering away from the land the DAKOTA headed straight towards it.

The Master was near the bow at the time and hurried back to the bridge to see what was happening. He then sent the Fourth Officer to the poop deck to find out what the helmsman was doing. It was already too late. The rocks were fast approaching and in desperation the master ordered 'Full Astern'. The DAKOTA hit the rocks with a disturbing grinding and ripping sound and her streamline bows reared up above the waves. Rockets were fired into the dark sky and the 218 passengers were soon

The DAKOTA aground on the East Mouse Rock in 1877.

being ferried to the shore by the Bull Bay Lifeboat.

The mail she was carrying, destined for New York, was then sent ashore while the crew remained aboard the wrecked ship.
The iron hull, four hundred feet long, was soon abandoned to the elements, but a large amount of the 2,000 ton general cargo was salvaged before the DAKOTA slipped onto her side and disappeared beneath the waves.

There was a Court of Inquiry at Liverpool where the court suspected that there was a cover-up to protect the helmsman. Those giving evidence stuck to their story that, despite the fact that the wheel was turned correctly, the ship refused to turn to starboard.

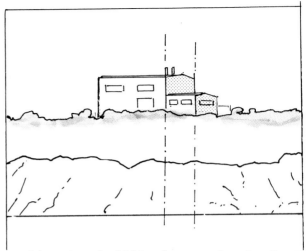

Looking South (190 C) towards the land. West gable-end of the larger Industrial building fits above the northern elevation of the smaller building.

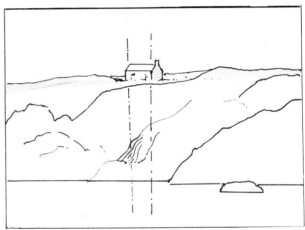

View East South East (120 C) to the headland beyond Amlwch Harbour. A grey house is directly above the waterfall from a discharge pipe.

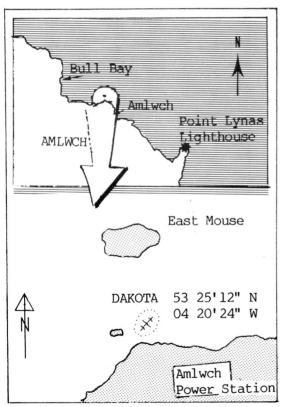

Wreck lies 30 metres North East of a rock that dries at low water

DIVE DETAILS
Location: 53°25'12" N 04°20'24" W
Depth: 15m to 22m
Seabed: pebbles & coarse gravel
Currents: v.strong, care required
Underwater Visibility: good
Launch Site: Amlwch or Bull Bay

DAKOTIAN

Type: Merchant Ship
Port of Registry: Liverpool
Tonnage: 6,426 tons gross
Built: 1922, Glasgow
Length: 400 feet
Breadth: 52 feet
Date of Sinking: November 21st 1940
Location: Milford Haven, Pembrokeshire
          Dyfed

The natural harbour of Milford Haven was a prime target for enemy attacks during World War II. Mines dropped by aircraft parachuted down onto its waters in November 1940 and were to cause a series of ship losses in the following few days and the intended confusion. One of the losses was the large Liverpool merchant ship DAKOTIAN. She was leaving the Haven when the Captain was advised to return by the authorities due to enemy activity in the sea area immediately outside St Ann's Head.

The DAKOTION was carrying a cargo of tinplate and a variety of other goods which included bicycles and Christmas puddings. The ship was anchoring in Dale Roads and had just let go one of her anchors when there was a terrific explosion. A magnetic mine had been activated by her hull and a huge hole was blown out of her side. She began to sink quickly.

Those that were in their bunks were hurried onto the deck and the lifeboats were hastily

manned but the ship sank within three minutes and some of the men were forced to jump over the side into the water wearing only their pyjamas. One of the crew who found himself in the water, swam for the shore, a distance of over half a mile. Covered in oil from head to foot he stumbled ashore and got a lift to Milford where his relations lived. The patrol boats spent all night searching the sea for him, the only person not accounted for. He was enjoying a warm bath and a hot meal, and had completely forgotten to inform the authorities of his safety!

The following day the 3,683 ton steamship PIKEPOOL was sunk by a mine outside the Haven and a few days later mines were responsible for a further two losses within the Haven; the 630 ton salvage vessel PRESERVER and the 6,100 ton steamship BEHAR.

WRECK POSITION
1 West Blockhouse in line with red cliffs at Lindsway Bay
2 Watwick Beacon in line with Beacon near Sandy Haven
3 Field edge left of Monk Haven in line with East Blockhouse
4 Radio Mast, towards Milford Haven bears 100 C

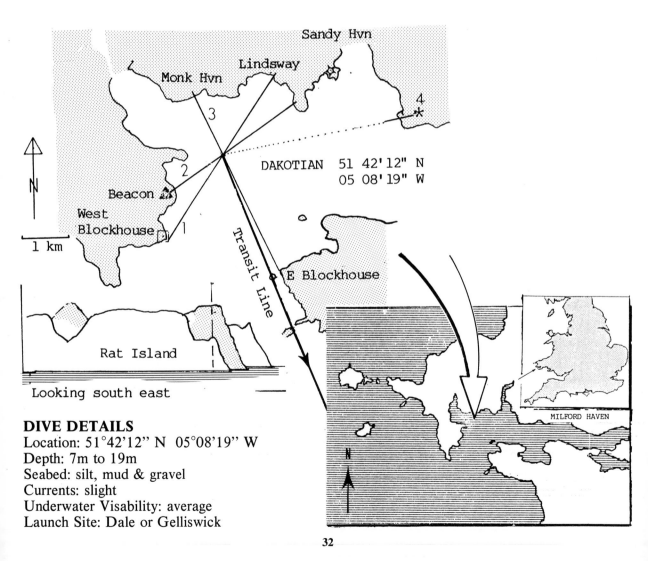

DIVE DETAILS
Location: 51°42'12" N 05°08'19" W
Depth: 7m to 19m
Seabed: silt, mud & gravel
Currents: slight
Underwater Visability: average
Launch Site: Dale or Gelliswick

DAN BEARD

Type: Liberty Ship
Port of Registry: San Francisco
Tonnage: 7176 tons gross
Built: 1943, California, USA
Length: 423 feet
Breadth: 57 feet
Date of Sinking: December 10th 1944
Location: Near Strumble Head,
               Pembrokeshire, Dyfed

During the first nine months of World War II the U-boats were sinking ships faster than the British shipyards could build them. Britain needed vital supplies and that required sea transport which was becoming impossible to acquire. One hundred and fifty dry cargo ships had been lost by enemy action during the first year of the war and the need to build merchantmen was acute. America with her neutrality and being beyond the range of the German bomber planes seemed an obvious place to build the much needed bulk carrying vessels.

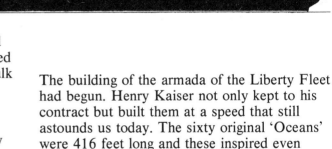

There were snags; America did not have the shipyards or the shipbuilding skills. What they did have, however, was a Mr Henry J Kaiser, a character with a remarkable organising ability.

Unknown in the shipbuilding industry he took on the contract to build the first sixty ships for Britain. In the winter of 1940 Richmond, California consisted of a few scattered houses and vast expanses of mudbank. It was there that Mr Kaiser decided to build thirty of the ships and he had signed to deliver them two years later.

In just four months the place was transformed into one of the world's most productive shipyards. 25,000 piles were driven into the mud to produce a massive factory where seven ships could be built simultaneously, and the keel of the first 'Ocean' ship had already started.

The building of the armada of the Liberty Fleet had begun. Henry Kaiser not only kept to his contract but built them at a speed that still astounds us today. The sixty original 'Oceans' were 416 feet long and these inspired even bigger ships. So streamlined did the shipbuilding process become that the time taken to build, from laying of the keel to the ship's launch, was just thirty two days.

During 1943, the Permanente Metal Corporation built the DAN BEARD, 7,176 tons, in Yard No.2 at Richmond. Her engines were built at the Joshua Henry Ironworks, Sunnyvale, California. These ships were collectively known as Liberty Ships and were of an all welded construction with an intended lifespan of five years.

The DAN BEARD'S life ended the following year when she was hit by an an underwater explosion. U.1202, an enemy submarine lying in wait in the shipping channel off Strumble Head had fired a torpedo with deadly accuracy. The huge ship lurched and broke into two killing 29 men. The two sections of the ship remained afloat for most of the day until the stern section sank in deep water. The St David's Lifeboat rescued 12 men and others saved themselves by coming ashore in the ship's lifeboats.

The bow section of the DAN BEARD drifted ashore beneath a sheer cliff at Pwllderi. Sections of her foremast and winch parts can still be seen at low water lying amongst the rocks.

Mast and bow winch of the DAN BEARD.

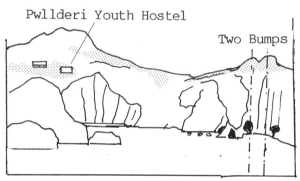

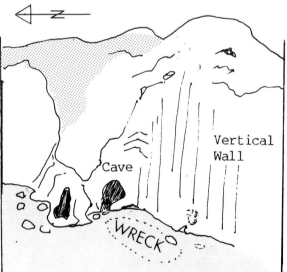

View looking South East (120°C) into Pwllderi. Look for 2 bumps on the headland top to right of the bay. Beneath is a vertical cliff wall. At the base of this wall are 2 tiny rock pinnacles surrounded by water. The wreck lies between these and the large cave in the corner.

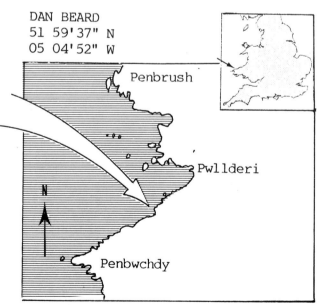

DIVE DETAILS
Location: 51°59'37" N 05°04'52" W
Depth: 8m to 13m
Seabed: rock & kelp
Currents: none
Underwater Visibility: good
Launch Site: Goodwick or Abercastle

DUISBERG

Type: Sailing Ship, Barque rigged
Port of Registry: Christiania, Norway
Tonnage: 1,040 tons gross
Built: 1856, Vegesack
Length: 183 feet
Breadth: 35 feet
Date of Sinking: November 13th 1899
Location: Oxwich Point, Gower

The last voyage of the DUISBERG was one which her master, Captain Olsen, was never to forget. The three-masted barque left Parsboro, Nova Scotia, with a cargo of timber (spruce and birch deal) destined for Swansea. The DUISBERG was an elderly vessel of forty three years old, and she was prone to some water seeping into her hull which prompted her owners to fit a windmill pump to help keep her dry.

Soon after leaving the Canadian coast the DUISBERG developed a leak which was such a bad one that Captain Olsen and the whole crew had to manually pump out throughout the voyage in order to survive.

The Atlantic journey was a hectic one. They attempted to put into the Azores but adverse winds prevented this. They then thought of getting into Cork harbour but also

The DUISBERG quietly at anchor, the men in the rigging having time to wave at the camera.

failed. Apart from being fatigued with pumping, they were running desperately low on food as the journey had taken them sixty days instead of the usual thirty.

When entering the Bristol Channel the ship became unmanageable and they were forced to jettison the timber deck cargo overboard. As the ship approached Port Eynon she was out of control, and those watching thought that the ship had been abandoned as she drifted up the channel broadside on. The DUISBERG came in near the Sandy Buoy and drove bows-on to the rocks near Oxwich Point. The fore and main masts toppled soon after she struck. Fortunately the 24 crew had already left the wreck in the ship's boat which was then guided into a safe landing near Oxwich Church by the Coastguards waiting on the shore. The DUISBERG was left high and dry when the tide receded allowing the men to recover their possessions and later for the successful salvage of the timber cargo.

The DUISBERG was owned by George Anderson of Christiania, Norway, who was not insured for the loss.

ELLERBECK

Type: Cargo Steamship
Port of Registry: Newcastle
Official Number: 129757
Tonnage: 1,499 tons gross
Built: 1910
Length: 245 feet
Breadth: 36 feet
Engines: 224 nhp
Date of Sinking: August 15th 1914
Location: Hats & Barrels, Pembrokeshire
Dyfed

Barrels Rock is remote; it is an underwater reef situated between Grassholm and the Smalls and is some fourteen miles from the entrance to Milford Haven. A similar rock called the Hats is two miles seaward and the area is termed the Hats and Barrels. It is curious why they are so named and it may be because in days gone by wreckage in the form of barrels and personal belongings such as hats were seen floating in the vicinity. There is little doubt that this area has claimed numerous victims throughout the centuries and even in recent times have caused casualties; such as the coaster LUMINENCE in 1967, oil tankers CHRISTOS BITAS in 1978 and BRIDGENESS in 1985.
The Barrels only shows itself above the waves occasionally.

The ELLERBECK went aground in August 1914, just ten days after war had been

The ELLERBECK aground on the Barrels Rock. Later she slipped off the rock and sank into deep water.

declared. On Admiralty service, she had collected a cargo of 2,000 tons of coal at Barry, and was bound for the Pentland Firth. On impact with the submerged reef her hull was badly damaged forward and a rock had pierced into the engine room. Signals of distress were seen on the mainland and the St David's Lifeboat, GENERAL FARRELL, went out to her assistance. Fortunately the weather was calm and some of the steamer's crew took to the boats and were met by the Lifeboat. Although the forepart was waterlogged the Captain asked for volunteers to remain on board in case there was a chance of getting her off with a subsequent high tide. 10 men and Captain Hay stayed while the Lifeboat took 8 men ashore together with all their belongings, and some of the ship's effects including the ship's gramophone.

The Milford trawler AVONMOUTH arrived later to find the stranded ELLERBECK rocking gently back and forth perched on top of the barrels reef. The remaining crew shouted across to the trawler that they wished to be taken off. They abandoned the stricken steamer and were taken safely to Milford by a fishing smack.

Captain Hay of the ELLERBECK was one of the firm's oldest and most trusted masters and when he was questioned about the experience he recalled that he was responsible for rescuing a shipwrecked crew in the same spot some ten years before.

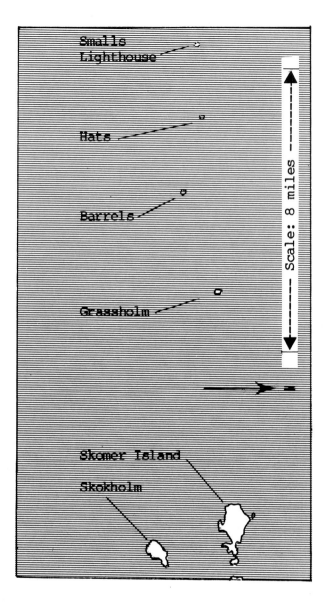

FARADAY

Type: Steamer, Cable Layer
Port of Registry: London
Official Number: 68535
Tonnage: 2,934 tons net
Built: 1874
Length: 360 feet
Breadth: 52 feet
Engines: 4 cylinder, 536 nhp
Date of Sinking: March 26th 1941
Location: Hooper's Point, St Ann's Head,
            Pembrokeshire, Dyfed

Enemy action caused the loss of the large cable ship FARADAY . She had a cargo of 3,870 tons of submarine cable on a voyage from Falmouth to Milford Haven when an enemy aircraft spotted her only a few miles outside St Ann's Head.

The FARADAY was bombed and set on fire by the Luftwaffe only a few miles outside the sanctuary of the Haven and the ship, still burning, drifted ashore. There was a terrible loss of life; out of the crew of 125, 16 lost their lives.

The survivors abandoned the ship, some manning the lifeboats and others were taken off by a Belgian trawler which also managed to tow the lifeboats nearer to the coast. The trawler was not allowed to enter the Haven during darkness hours so the men were transferred to the Angle Lifeboat which took 56 survivors ashore.

The FARADAY remained on fire until the following day when the wreck sank under the cliffs of Hooper's Point near West Dale. The cargo was a valuable wartime commodity and no less than ninety miles of submarine cable was successfully salvaged from the wreck.

Divers are alerted to the fact that this wreck may be designated a 'protected place' under the Military Remains Act 1986. If diving is allowed then the FARADAY is an interesting

Telegraph face, spoon and brass frame from the FARADAY.

and worthwhile site to dive on. It is easy to locate, very shallow, and simple to anchor above. As an added bonus there is often very good visibility on the site.

Although there is a strong current sixty metres away, the wreckage lying immediately beneath the cliffs does not seem to be affected by currents.

DIVE DETAILS

Location: 51°42'40" N 05°12'12" W
Depth: 5m to 16m
Seabed: rock & gravel
Currents: none (close in)
Underwater visibility: good
Launch Site: Dale

The cable layer FARADAY burning beneath Hooper's Point after being bombed by an enemy aircraft.

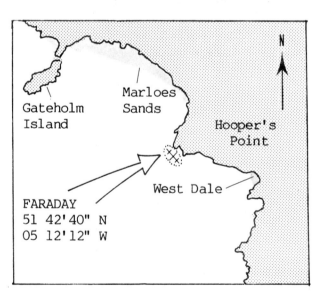

Gateholm
Island

Marloes
Sands

Hooper's
Point

West Dale

FARADAY
51 42'40" N
05 12'12" W

N

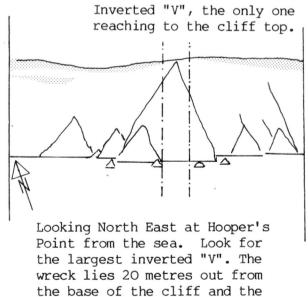

Inverted "V", the only one
reaching to the cliff top.

Looking North East at Hooper's
Point from the sea. Look for
the largest inverted "V". The
wreck lies 20 metres out from
the base of the cliff and the
sharp rocks.

FLYING FOAM

Type: Sailing Vessel, Schooner Rigged
Port of Registry: Bridgewater
Tonnage: 112 tons gross
Length: 88 feet
Breadth: 20 feet
Built: 1879, Jersey
Date of Sinking: June 21st 1936
Location: North of Deganwy, Llandudno
Gwynedd

The FLYING FOAM, a Bridgewater schooner, was laden with a full cargo of coal when she found herself off the north Wales coast in worsening weather.

She anchored between Puffin Island and Penmaenmawr in order to repair a sail on June 21st 1936. Built in the Channel Islands at Jersey the schooner was somewhat aged at fifty seven years old.

The anchor failed to hold and the FLYING FOAM slowly dragged across Conway Bay towards the shore. The Beaumaris Lifeboat was informed of her plight and chased after her and successfully rescued the 7 crew. Trawlermen from Conway tried to salvage the schooner by climbing aboard and pumping her out but the waves drove the FLYING FOAM onto the beach and her hull was broken beyond repair.

A Llandudno coal merchant was quick to take every advantage of the situation and soon purchased the wreck and the coal cargo as it lay on the beach. The photograph shows his men unloading the cargo using a wooden chute to extract the coal from the hold, and a number of horses and carts to move as much coal as possible before the next incoming tide.

The remnants of this vessel can still be seen at low water beyond the West Shore car park.

FROLIC

Type: Paddle Steamer
Port of Registry: Bristol
Tonnage: 108 tons old measurement
Built: 1827, Glasgow
Length: 112 feet
Breadth: 18 feet
Date of Sinking: March 16th 1831
Location: Nash Sands, Porthcawl,
           Glamorgan

In 1830 ten enterprising Bristol businessmen purchased a small schooner-rigged paddle steamer from the noted Glasgow shipbuilder John Scott. Their purchase was FROLIC a two masted vessel of wooden carvel construction of 108 tons with a square stern. The joint owners were part of the Bristol General Steam Packet Company and had bought her to start a new packet service between Bristol and West Wales.

In those pre-railway days it was an important link not only to West Wales but also with Irish trade entering and leaving Milford Haven. She commenced her new routine run in the autumn and the people of Carmarthen had their first sighting of a steamer on the river Towy on November 25th 1830.

A poster dated December 1830 described the FROLIC as a new vessel of nearly 100 horse power and was 'Announced to sail between Bristol and Carmarthen, calling off at Tenby when practicable, to land and receive passengers, and between Bristol and Haverfordwest, taking goods for Milford and Pembroke Dock, at shipper's risk.' The cost of a cabin was just over £1, the cost of taking a horse and two wheeled carriage £2.50p and a dog 15p.

It is interesting to note that there is a riverside walkway at Haverfordwest named 'The Frolic' where this vessel probably took on its passengers.

In March 1831 the FROLIC, with Captain Edward Jenkins in command was returning to Bristol from Haverfordwest. She was making her way round Nash Point when she struck hard into a sandbank. There were no survivors and the exact numbers on board were never ascertained but it was thought that about 55 people were lost.

There were at least 40 passengers including some high ranking Officers and one General as well as some important Pembrokeshire merchants. The public outcry which followed the disaster prompted the planning and building of two lighthouses on Nash Point.

Designed by James Walker, the Engineer-in-Chief of Trinity House, two massive circular lighthouses were completed in 1832.

NASH LIGHTHOUSES

The building of the two Lighthouses at Nash Point was as a direct result of ship losses on the Nash Sands, and, in particular, to avoid tragedies similar to the one in 1831, when the paddle steamer FROLIC was lost with all on board.

Two massive stone circular lighthouses were constructed, 1000 feet (about 300 metres) apart. The western lighthouse is the lower one and has always been painted white. The eastern or higher lighthouse used to be painted black and white but today is all white and displays a light, group flashing (2) white and red every ten seconds, which can be seen twenty-one miles away. Both lighthouses originally had fixed white lights which, if kept in line, would lead the vessel safely to the south of the notorious Nash Sands.

The 1868 Sailing Directions give the following advice about Nash Lighthouses; 'Masters of vessels sailing up the Bristol Channel, in the fairway, will make these as two separate and distinct lights; while, to prevent the possibility of mistaking them for those of St Ann's Point (Milford Haven), it should be observed, that in making the lights upon the Nash Point from the

The Nash Lighthouses have helped mariners to keep clear of the Nash Sands since the FROLIC disaster in 1831.

south-westward, the high light will be seen to the right, or southward of the low light; whereas, in making St Ann's lights from the same quarter, the high light will be seen to the left, or northward of the low light'. It continues, 'When these lights are in line, they will lead southward of the sands lying westward of the point'.

Nash Sands extends six and a half miles north west of Nash Point and the same book warns No vessel ought to approach any part of the Sands, except with a smooth sea'.

GRAFFOE

Type: Cargo Steamship Port of
Registry: Grimsby Official
Number: 99681
Tonnage: 2,996 tons gross
Built: 1892, West Hartlepool
Length: 314 feet
Breadth: 40 feet
Date of Sinking: January 25th 1903
Location: Near Ramsey Is., St David's,
　　　　　　Pembrokeshire, Dyfed

The Grimsby steamer GRAFFOE left Glasgow on January 23rd 1903, and was bound for the South American port of Montevideo, heavily laden with a cargo of coal. A storm in the Irish Sea caused her steering gear to fail and she was driven out of control towards St David's.

It was in darkness on January 25th that the GRAFFOE hit the rocks at the southern end of Ramsey Sound and for the crew it was the beginning of a traumatic experience. Fourteen of the crew manned one of the ship's lifeboats which managed to get away from the sinking ship. The men tried to keep this boat near to the wreck but found the task impossible in the heavy seas and ebbing current of the Sound. It was swept south and was discovered the next day by a passing steamer. The survivors were all picked up and landed at Penarth. They were the lucky ones, those left on the wreck were to experience greater distress and hardship.

The GRAFFOE slowly broke up in the swell and the remaining crew failed to launch the second ship's boat. They were forced to find shelter in the bridge or the rigging as her decks were awash.

The GRAFFOE had been holed and had sunk to the seabed ten metres below, leaving only the upper part of the bridge clear of the waves which swept over her continuously. The Captain and the Chief Engineer were washed overboard and drowned.

The bitter January storm continued and there were 7 men still remaining on the sunken steamer. They lashed themselves to the rigging hoping that their plight would be seen by someone on the mainland. All night they waited in vain but no one ashore knew of the shipwreck to raise the alarm; the St David's Lifeboat GEM lay dormant in the Lifeboathouse two miles away. The hopes of the men in the rigging were raised during the next day when they saw a figure on the mainland cliff opposite.

Thinking it must be a Coastguard Officer they were heartened but the truth of the matter was that they had sighted a farm boy who had still failed to see their dilemma. The shipwrecked crew were forced to cling with frozen hands for a further night before they were seen at 10am the next morning.

The Lifeboat GEM was launched and was rowed across Ramsey Sound. For one man, rescue came too late, his body was the first to be taken off, testing the line to the Lifeboat. It was remarkable that any of the men were still alive, they had survived two winter nights and a day clinging to the sunken ship.

The lucky 6 survivors were taken back to St David's. One of them was later to write to the press saying he had seen a Coastguard on the cliffs during his ordeal and claiming that the authorities had neglected their duty. The RNLI were certainly impressed with the rescue and awarded a silver medal to the St David's Lifeboat Coxswain, William Narbett.

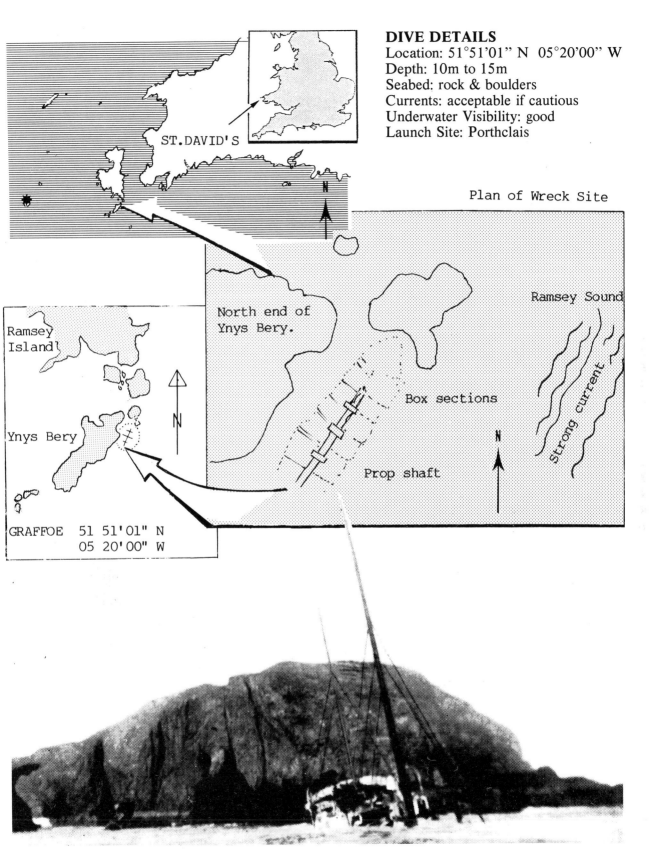

DIVE DETAILS
Location: 51°51'01" N 05°20'00" W
Depth: 10m to 15m
Seabed: rock & boulders
Currents: acceptable if cautious
Underwater Visibility: good
Launch Site: Porthclais

ST.DAVID'S

N

Plan of Wreck Site

Ramsey Sound

North end of
Ynys Bery.

Box sections

Strong current

Prop shaft

N

Ramsey
Island

Ynys Bery

N

GRAFFOE 51 51'01" N
          05 20'00" W

Wreck of the GRAFFOE.

GRAMSBERGEN

Type: Coasting Cargo Vessel
Port of Registry: Rotterdam
Tonnage: 498 tons gross
Built: 1954
Date of Sinking: November 28th 1954
Location: Fishguard, Pembrokeshire,
        Dyfed

The coaster GRAMSBERGEN was on a voyage from Cumberland to Swansea, in ballast, when she entered the bay at Fishguard.

Her Captain, J.L.Van Dulleman, had anticipated a bad storm and was looking for shelter. His ship was almost brand new, being only six months old and he anchored her near to the harbour entrance. The harbour launch

soon came over informing him that he had anchored in the middle of the fairway and advised him to move his vessel three lengths to port.

This was done but at 1.50am a heavy swell broke the anchor chain and the coaster went drifting madly across the bay. Before the engineers had time to start the engines the ship

Wreckage of the GRAMSBERGEN lying on the rock and sand seabed at ten metres depth. This photograph (by the author) was shot using natural light only, but visibility at the site is not often this good.

The Dutch coaster GRAMSBERGEN broke from her anchorage and was wrecked in Fishguard Bay in 1954. This photograph shows her beneath Penrhyn Point shortly before she sank.

had hit the rocks. The GRAMSBERGEN
landed beneath Penrhyn but a reef of rocks
prevented her from sinking immediately.

There were 11 crew on board the stranded
coaster. One of the Dutch seamen offered to
swim a line to the cliffs forty metres away. The
twenty two year old crewman successfully got a
line ashore and was helped up the cliff by a
local farmer, but within an hour the Fishguard
Lifeboat was alongside. The weather was
atrocious and the Lifeboat took the crew and
Captain off the wreck but when they tried to
leave, a rope had caught and fouled the
Lifeboat's propeller. The harbour launch,
PENCW, herself an ex RNLI Lifeboat, had to
be called upon to tow the Fishguard Lifeboat to
the quayside.

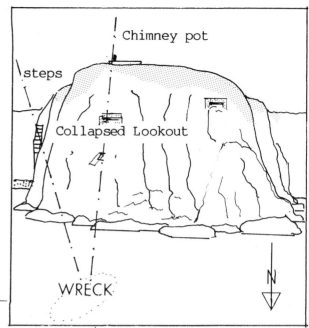

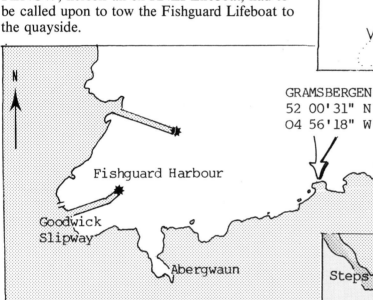

GRAMSBERGEN
52 00'31" N
04 56'18" W

DIVE DETAILS
Location: 52°00'31" N
           04°56'18" W
Depth: 6m to 14m
Seabed: rock, gravel & sand
Currents: weak
Underwater Visibility: fair, poor
                        in NW
Launch Site: Goodwick or
             Pwllgwaelod

All the crew and the ship's mascots, two six
week old puppies, were safely landed but the
GRAMSBERGEN later sank into eleven
metres of water.

How to find the GRAMSBERGEN.
Launch at Goodwick (neaps & HW are
best). Outer Breakwater points
to Penrhyn (caravan site). On the
North East corner of Penrhyn are steps
up the cliff. Go seawards 40m until
the roof of a building comes into view
above the left hand lookout. The top
of the steps can be seen but not the
lower half. White buildings at
Pwllgwaelod should be just out of sight.

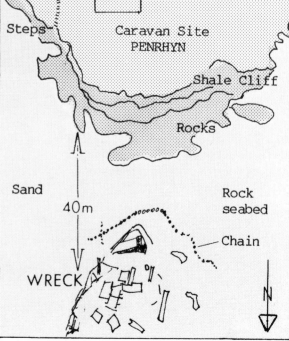

HAROLD

Type: Cargo Steamer
Port of Registry: Liverpool
Tonnage: 301 tons gross
Length: 140 feet
Breadth: 23 feet
Date of Sinking: February 22nd 1908
Location: Gogarth Bay, Holyhead,
       Ynys Mon

A February storm brought out the Holyhead steam Lifeboat DUKE OF NORTHUMBERLAND. Her task was to help the Liverpool steamer BENCROY that had broken down near the breakwater. The Lifeboat got to her and assisted by passing a tow rope from the disabled ship to another vessel that was then able to tow the BENCROY into the harbour.

No sooner had the Lifeboat returned to her anchorage than she was called out again; this time to a much more difficult assignment and it was to become one of the most courageous rescues in the history of the Holyhead Lifeboats.

The steamer in distress was the HAROLD belonging to Mr T.Best of the Liverpool Lighterage Co.. With a cargo of 290 tons of clay she was on her way from Teignmouth to Runcorn when her engine broke down five miles off the coast. It was at the height of a full west south west gale and she quickly drifted towards the South Stack, flying her ensign upside down as a signal of distress. The Barrow steamer SOUND FISHER noticed her plight and tried to get a line aboard, but failed. The HAROLD'S two anchors were dropped and the 9 crewmen huddled together on the bridge hoping the anchors would hold. They tried lowering the ship's boat but it was soon smashed to pieces, fortunately before anyone had climbed into it. The men were now trapped on board with the steamer getting dangerously close to huge cliffs with enormous seas breaking all round them; luckily the anchors held.

The Lifeboat showed up and made an attempt to get alongside, her Coxswain, William Owen was experiencing the worst conditions he had ever seen. The entire area was a mass of white foam and the waves buffeted both vessels like bobbing corks. The task seemed hopeless. Each time the Lifeboat got near the waves would hurl her away and it took almost two hours of determination before the Lifeboat could get close enough for a rope to be thrown. A pulley was set up and 6 men were taken off, being hauled through the water. The Lifeboat was then taken close enough for the remaining men to jump across.

Leaving the HAROLD at anchor under the steep cliffs of Gogarth the Lifeboat returned to Holyhead and the survivors were greeted with a warm meal at the Sailors' Home in front of a roaring fire.

The abandoned HAROLD foundered the next morning midway between the Stacks and despite some dispersal by Trinity House still provides an interest for divers.

Coxswain Owen was awarded an RNLI gold medal for this outstanding rescue and the entire Lifeboat crew were each awarded a silver medal.

DIVE DETAILS
Location: 53°18'38" N 04°41'33" W
Depth: 10m to 14m
Seabed: gravel
Currents: 1-2 knots
Underwater Visibility: fair
Launch Site: Holyhead or Porth Dafarch

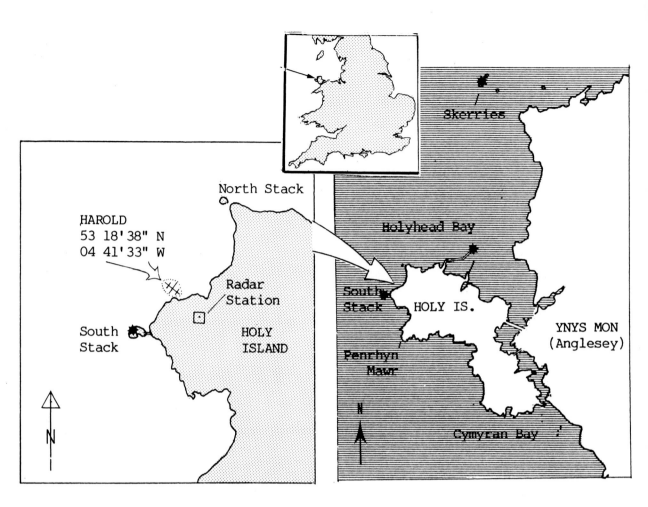

HAROLD
53 18'38" N
04 41'33" W

North Stack

Radar
Station

HOLY
ISLAND

South
Stack

N

Skerries

Holyhead Bay

South
Stack

HOLY IS.

YNYS MON
(Anglesey)

Penrhyn
Mawr

N

Cymyran Bay

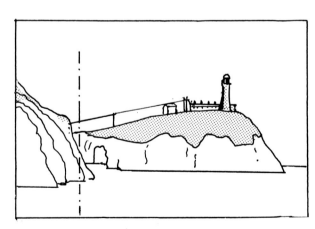

View South West (225°C) towards
South Stack Lighthouse. Look for
the pole where the electricity
lines start rising (over the
bridge). Transit is when this
pole is just hidden by the cliff.

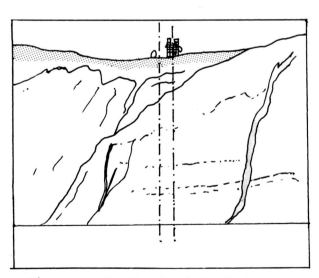

View towards the land South East
(130°C). The Radar dishes are
positioned between two large cracks
in the nearest headland.

HEREFORDSHIRE

Type: Steamer, Twin Screw, 4 Masted
Port of Registry: Liverpool
Official Number: 120903
Tonnage: 5,905 tons gross
Built: 1905, Belfast
Length: 452 feet
Breadth: 54 feet
Date of Sinking: March 15th 1934
Location: Cardigan Island, Dyfed

The Smith Shipbreaking Company had purchased the liner HEREFORDSHIRE for scrap from the Bibby Steamship Company and now had the task of towing it to Glasgow from where it had lain in Dartmouth. Two Glasgow tugs, CHIEFTAIN and WRESTLER were hired to carry out the tow. Bad weather caused the small convoy to shelter in Falmouth. After a few days they set off in fair conditions only to find the weather deteriorating rapidly. At Strumble Head they met big seas and hurricane force winds. The towing hawser to the WRESTLER broke at 2.30pm on March 14th, 1934, and although every effort was made to reconnect, this was impossible in the huge seas. Just over twelve hours later the second hawser parted leaving the disabled liner and her crew of 4 men to drift ashore.

The tugs sent out SOS signals and the Fishguard Lifeboat went out but failed to sight her. The Cardigan Coastguards reported that the HEREFORDSHIRE had gone aground on Cardigan Island. The Gwbert Lifesaving Crew were at the ready on the mainland cliffs and there was a sigh of relief when the four survivors were seen on the top of the island. A rocket line was fired with great accuracy across Cardigan Sound and one by one the men were hauled through the water by Breeches Buoy to the mainland cliffs. As the first man emerged from the icy water he was heard to chatter 'that was the coldest quarter mile I can remember!.'

The entire ship's furnishings were on board when she was lost and many of the fittings, cutlery and linen were later auctioned.

One crewman is hauled to safety.

The HEREFORDSHIRE before she broke up.

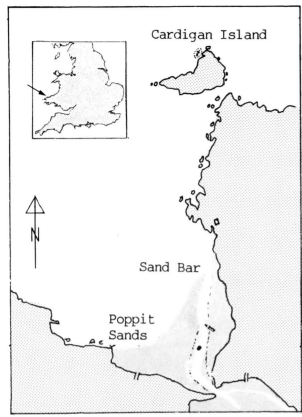

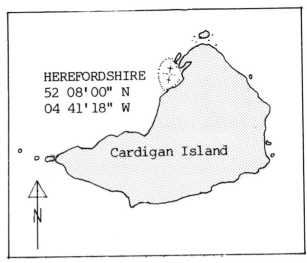

HEREFORDSHIRE
52 08'00" N
04 41'18" W

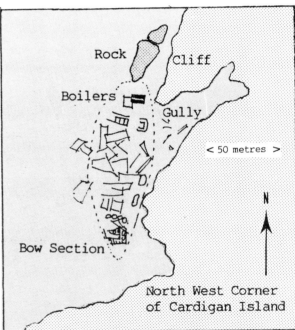

Launch at St Dogmaels about half an
hour before HW at Milford Haven, this
is well before the Teifi floods and will
give you about an hour and half on the
wreck site before returning. Otherwise
you may find difficulty returning when
the tide is out. Beware of dangerous
overfalls on the sand bar half way between
the Perch and the Cliff Hotel.

The wreck on the rocks of Cardigan Island.

In the 1930's there was an established puffin
colony on Cardigan Island, but within a few
years of the HEREFORDSHIRE sinking they
had all disappeared, their burrows having
become infested with rats that had deserted the
sinking ship. Only now, fifty years later, have
puffins started to return to the island to breed.

DIVE DETAILS
Location: 52°08'00" N 04°41'18" W
Depth: 5m to 11m
Seabed: Rock & shingle
Currents: none; but bad swells
Underwater Visibility: poor
Launch Site: St Dogmaels, Cardigan

HERMINA

Type: Sailing, 3 Masted Schooner
Port of Registry: Rotterdam
Date of Sinking: December 3rd 1920
Location: Needle Rock, Fishguard Bay,
            Pembrokeshire, Dyfed

The Dutch motor schooner HERMINA was returning to her home port of Rotterdam when she ran into Fishguard to take shelter from a strong north-west gale. Her anchors started to drag and Captain Vooitgedacht ordered a distress flare to be fired as he feared for the safety of the 10 man crew.

It was already dark when the Fishguard motor Lifeboat CHARTERHOUSE sped across the bay. The Lifeboat's Coxswain was John Howells and, nearing sixty six years of age, he was about to perform one of the most famous of all Welsh rescues.

The Lifeboat anchored about one hundred metres to windward of the distressed schooner and veered alongside by paying out the anchor warp. Tremendous seas swept across both vessels and they had great difficulty in securing a line to the schooner. The seas lifted the Lifeboat right into the ship's rigging and it took an hour of strenuous effort to get 7 men off. The Captain, Chief Officer and the Second Mate refused to get off the schooner despite the pleading from Coxswain Howells who knew that the vessel would break up on the rocks if it dragged any more.

During the rescue the Lifeboat was drenched and the engine refused to start when they wanted to head for home. It was a desperate situation and they had to rely on the oars, sails and their seamanship to get away from the sheer cliffs behind them. No sooner had they raised the anchor than the mizzen sail was caught by the wind, it was ripped to pieces and was lost overboard. The men were now in trouble. Two lifeboatmen climbed onto the bow of the Lifeboat and managed to set the jib sail while the port oars manouvered the boat so that it could tack away from the cliffs. They

sailed out to sea for two miles before they had enough searoom to sail back to the Goodwick harbour. In all, it took them three hours to return. No sooner had they reached the quayside than more flares were seen from the direction of the HERMINA.

It was impossible to return by sea and the only hope of rescue for the 3 men lay with the cliff rescue team. The schooner rapidly hit Needle

The only known picture of the HERMINA breaking up beneath Needle Rock.

Rock and immediately broke apart; one of the men was washed away and drowned. The Captain and Chief Officer succeeded in reaching the base of the cliff where they were both rescued by the courageous William Morgan who was lowered by rope to save them.

The Dutch Government awarded silver pocket watches to the entire Lifeboat crew in appreciation; Coxswain Howells and William Morgan received gold watches. The RNLI also showed their gratitude by awarding medals to all the Lifeboatmen, and to John Howells their highest honour, a gold medal. So proud were the Lifeboatmen that in April 1921 they took themselves, complete with their Lifeboat, on the train to London, to present themselves to the Duke of Windsor, President of the RNLI.

Cox John Howells who was awarded a Lifeboat VC.

Above: The Lifeboat CHARTERHOUSE, one of the first RNLI Lifeboats with an engine. At Fishguard from 1908 to 1930 she saved 47 lives.

Left: One of the watches awarded to the Lifeboat crew by the Dutch Government.

Below: The Duke of Windsor inspects the Fishguard Lifeboat, especially taken to London for the presentation of the awards.

JAMES GRAY

Type: Cargo Steamship
Port of Registry: Whitby
Official Number: 72140
Tonnage: 1,626 tons gross
Built: 1877, Whitby
Length: 256 feet
Breadth: 34 feet
Engines: 140 nhp
Date of Sinking: January 27th 1883
Location: Tusker Rock, near Porthcawl,
Glamorgan

A gale of tremendous proportions hit the Bristol Channel in January 1883. Its devastation, through shipwreck, caused the loss of at least 45 lives in the Swansea Bay area alone. The Liverpool steamer AGNES JACK was lost off Oxwich with the loss of 18 lives, and 5 were drowned when the AMIRAL PRINZ ADALBERT came ashore near Mumbles Lighthouse, two of them belonging to the Mumbles Lifeboat crew. On Tusker Rock, off Porthcawl, the entire crew and passengers of the steamer JAMES GRAY were lost despite attempts to save them by the Porthcawl Lifeboat.

The JAMES GRAY, owned by J.Gray & Co. and laden with a cargo of Cardiff coal, had set out for the Cape Verde Islands when the storm hit. The steamer was seen in distress on the Fairy Bank, about two miles east of Porthcawl, she was dragging anchor with her steering or machinery out of order. A very heavy sea was running but the Porthcawl Lifeboat launched to the rescue. Once outside the breakwater the Lifeboat found the seas too rough and the Coxswain decided to take the Lifeboat to Newton Pool where the crew waited until a tugboat could return them to base.

At 8pm. two rockets were fired from the JAMES GRAY as she crashed onto the notorious Tusker Rock. After that nothing was seen of life aboard the wreck and all who witnessed the conditions knew that no small boat would have survived in the surf. It was a terrible loss of life; all the crew of the JAMES GRAY, including Captain McCloud, his wife and child were all drowned. Although the wrecked steamer was visible on the south side of Tusker Rock it was some days before the identity of the vessel was known. Two days later a message from Swansea reported, 'wreckage visible at low water. Name unknown. Description schooner rigged; about 1,200 tons burthen; loaded, painted lead colour; fear crew

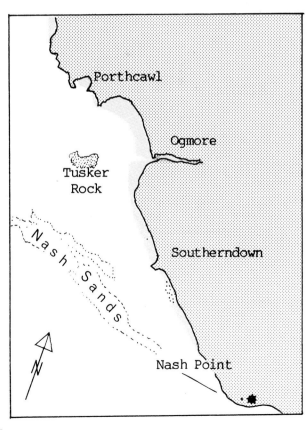

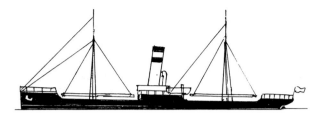

lost; two bodies reported found. A white burgee was picked up at Ogmore River with JAMES GRAY in red letters on it'. The following day a message from Southerndown reported that a body had been picked up and that it had been identified by a former Mate as that of Captain McCloud. Wreckage washed ashore between Ogmore and the Nash aswell as the bodies of two of the crew and the infant child of the Captain.

All 22 aboard the ship had lost their lives and such a disaster was to repeat itself three years later when the entire crew of the iron ship MALLENY was to hit the same reef in October 1886.

KIRKMICHAEL

Type: Steel Sailing Ship, Barque Rigged
Port of Registry: Liverpool
Official Number: 86269
Tonnage: 933 tons gross
Built: 1882, Sunderland
Length: 202 feet
Breadth: 33 feet
Date of Sinking: December 22nd 1894
Location: Holyhead Outer Breakwater,
          Ynys Mon

A December storm in 1894 caused chaos to shipping in Holyhead Bay. The full north-west gale caused ships to be driven onto the rocks and both Holyhead Lifeboats were battling with the seas trying to reach the shipwrecked crews.

The Norwegian barquentine VALHALLA , outward bound from Glasgow drove onto the rocks at Penrhos beach and the Lifeboat

THOMAS FIELDEN managed to save her 10 crew. Almost in the same place, later in the day, the Norwegian barque TITANIA was wrecked and her crew of 11 were saved by the No.2 Lifeboat JOSEPH WHITWORTH. On both these rescues the Lifeboats involved found conditions too bad to return and by the end of the day both Holyhead Lifeboats were beached near Penrhos.

Kirk Michael wrecked on Holyhead Breakwater December 23rd 1893. 4 Lives Lost

Earlier in the day the Lifeboat JOSEPH WHITWORTH was launched to rescue the crew of the barque KIRKMICHAEL that had been seen running into the harbour under bare poles, the barque eventually was driven against the seaward side of the breakwater. It was 10.30am when the Lifeboat crew launched into the teeth of the gale, and with each man straining at the oars they rowed across the bay. A big sea hit the Lifeboat, swamping it, and six oars were swept away. The lifeboatmen knew that they had to return to base. However the land based lifesaving team had already prepared themselves.

With frightening waves and wind estimated at over eighty miles per hour, the team had the dangerous task of getting to the far end of the breakwater. The only way was the arduous and difficult feat of crawling along dragging their gear behind them. With seas breaking continuously over them, they got to the KIRKMICHAEL and managed to fix a line to the stern. 11 men were taken off, including Captain Jones but 3 crew were still aboard. The Mate and Second Mate who were in the mizzen rigging refused to come ashore and also

the Steward who was in the cabin. Two of the rescue team went aboard to help off the men in the rigging but one mate fell and was killed and the other died from exposure before he could be got off.

11 men were saved, 7 men were lost and the Steward remained aboard. The Steward's judgement was a sound one for the following morning he was still alive and was then safely landed.

The KIRKMICHAEL, which was outward bound for Australia, was damaged beyond repair and her steel hull slipped off the rocks into ten metres of water where some of her remains can be seen today by divers.

DIVE DETAILS
Location: 53°19'30" N 04°37'12" W
Depth: 10m to 12m
Seabed: silt & rock
Currents: small, manageable all times
Underwater Visibility: average
Launch Site: Holyhead

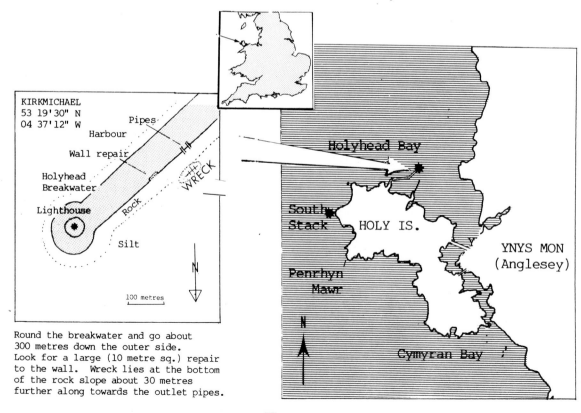

Round the breakwater and go about
300 metres down the outer side.
Look for a large (10 metre sq.) repair
to the wall. Wreck lies at the bottom
of the rock slope about 30 metres
further along towards the outlet pipes.

KITTY

Type: Sailing Ship, Full Rigged
Port of Registry: American
Tonnage: 300 tons
Date of Sinking: January 14th 1819
Location: Near Fishguard, Pembrokeshire, Dyfed

The weather in the second week of 1819 was atrocious and caused a great deal of suffering, loss of life and shipwrecks.

The western seaboard caught the worst of the west south west gale and ships were lost all along the coast. On January 9th the RANGER, Belfast to London, was driven on shore near Holyhead and two days later 3 crew, 3 passengers and the Master were drowned when the BETSEY, Waterford to Bristol, was wrecked on Traith Bar near Carmarthen.

On the same day the entire crew, except for the chief mate, was lost when the FRIENDSCHAFT, Liverpool to Havre, was driven on Malldraeth sands in Ynys Mon. Fortunately the ship was refloated at the end of the month.

The JOHN & CATHERINE, Teignmouth to Glasgow, foundered a few days later off the Smalls the weather actually having become more severe. The bad weather drove many ships further north than they anticipated which was the case with the VENERABLE, a 400 ton brig loaded with West African palm oil and ivory which came ashore at Newport, Dyfed.

The most intriguing of the stories comes from another large vessel of the day, the KITTY. With Captain Doggett in command the KITTY was completing the last leg of an Atlantic crossing when the gale hit. She had left Norfolk, Virginia, with a full cargo of tobacco and was destined for Falmouth when the winds forced them into the Irish Sea.

The gale smashed off her rudder and the full rigged ship developed a leak. They abandoned the 300 ton ship off Bardsey Island and the crew were saved by the MARMION, Leghorn to Liverpool, and were safely landed at Liverpool.

The KITTY was left to sink but she managed to stay afloat for the next three days and was then driven ashore near Fishguard on January 14th. As there was no-one aboard, the crew having already departed with the papers, there was a great deal of conjecture as to where the ship was heading and many people firmly beleived her to be a smuggler taking the tobacco to Southern Ireland. The tobacco cargo became strewn along several miles of coast near Fishguard and surrounding the wreck the sea turned to a yellow colour which poisoned the fish. We could say that records of ships' cargoes polluting the sea dates back to at least 1819!

KYLE FIRTH

Type: Coasting Steamer
Port of Registry: Glasgow
Previous Names: KYLE FORD,
                    OUISTREHAM,
                    SENGA
Tonnage: 450 tons gross
Length: 155 feet
Breadth: 26 feet
Date of Sinking: May 13th 1940
Location: Penrhyn Mawr, Ynys Mon

During World War II navigation was made more tricky by the absence of most of the beacon and lighthouse lights. They had been purposely extinguished in times of blackout to confuse the enemy but it also caused added hazards to local shipping. This was the case with the KYLE FIRTH, a coasting steamer that came to her end on the unlucky 13th of the month, May 1940.

On a calm black morning the KYLE FIRTH ran directly into the jagged headland of Penrhyn Mawr, just two miles south of the South Stack Lighthouse which had been extinguished. The Holyhead Lifeboat, A.E.D. went to her rescue and arrived to find that 4 men had already landed in the ship's boat. A further 5 men were taken off the coaster by the Lifeboat and they returned to Holyhead, abandoning the ship.

Throughout the war years the Holyhead Lifeboat was to perform thirty seven service launches and rescue seventy one lives, the Service record for this date being, 'Steamship KYLE FIRTH of Glasgow, saved a boat and 5'.

The KYLE FIRTH, which had previously had the names KYLE FORD, OUISTREHAM and SENGA, was taking a cargo of stone chippings from the quarry at Portnant to Liverpool when she was lost. Her steel remains and iron propellor are now found eleven metres below the waters off Penrhos Point.

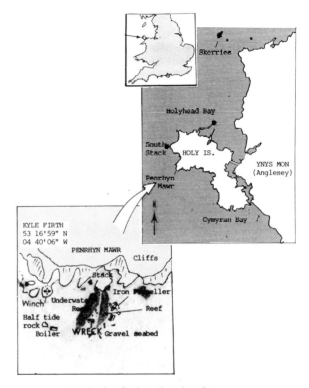

From Porth Dafarch go through rocks at Penrhos Point and keep close inshore. At Penrhyn Mawr look for a rock stack and a winch on the rocks beyond. A half tide rock lies just off the winch rock. The wreck lies between the half tide rock and the stack.

DIVE DETAILS

Location: 53°16'59" N 04°40'06" W
Depth: 9m to 15m
Seabed: rock, kelp & gravel
Currents: hazardous
Underwater Visibility: average
Launch Site: Porth Dafarch

LA JEUNE EMMA

Type: Sailing Ship, Brig Rigged.
    A French West Indiaman.
Port of Registry: Cherbourg, France
Tonnage: about 400 tons
Date of Sinking: November 21st 1828
Location: Cefn Sidan, Carmarthen Bay,
        Dyfed

French nobility was amongst those drowned in a tragic incident at Pembrey in 1828. LA JEUNE EMMA, a French brig was sailing from Fort Royal, Martinique to Le Havre, with a cargo of rum, sugar and coffee. Her Captain was under the mistaken impression that he was sailing along the coast of Finisterre. In fact he had seen the lights of Lundy and, thinking they belonged to the coast of Ushant had continued north. It was a fateful mistake and ended in so much controversy that it became one of Carmarthen Bay's most notorious shipwrecks.

A contemporary account of the story written a few weeks after the event is found in the Cambrian Quarterly;
'When she struck ...a scene of consternation and horror ensued which baffles description. The whole of the crew and passengers rushed on deck, over which the sea broke dreadfully, and before daylight 13 souls had been swept away by the breakers, and met a watery grave. The passengers were Colonel Coquelin, of the French Marines, and his daughter, an interesting young lady, neice to Josephine, 'ci-devant' Empress of France and consort of [Napoleon] Bonaparte, and their 2 servants, who all perished. 6 only were saved from a crew of 19. The assistance rendered to the few unfortunate survivors, needs no eulogism (praise) of ours. Commiseration for the exile and the stranger are always an honour to the nation in which they exist, particularly where it leads to a risk of life for the purpose of saving life. But what shall we say of those monsters, who, instead of succouring, robbed and ill-treated the helpless and perishing. What are we to think of wretches so dastardly as those who add cruelty and cowardice to avarice, and plunder only those whom the ocean has robbed of their strength. Do not these facts call for legislative interference ? Could not some mode be devised for enforcing the operation of existing laws ? This is but one instance of many !'

Memorial stone at Pembrey Church.

A pencil sketch drawn in Wales in 1827 of an unidentified square-rigged sailing ship being wrecked. It was conditions such as these the following year which caused the loss of thirteen lives when LA JEUNE EMMA was wrecked on Cefn Sidan.

When news of the wreck reached Carmarthen, members of the Royal Carmarthen Militia were immediately issued with cartridges and a good flint and ordered to march to Cefn Sidan, some fifteen miles away. By the time they had arrived to protect the wreck the looters had already done their worst.

One story, which emerged twenty years later, says that the twelve year old Adeline Coquelin had her fingers cut off to secure some rings. Another story describes a man who found a cask of rum on the shore, and, using a snuff box as a cup had drunk himself silly.

In Pembrey Parish Churchyard are buried nine of the thirteen people who lost their lives in the tragedy. On the lower portion of the Memorial stone are details of two other shipwrecks that have occurred on the same sands; The BROTHERS of Liverpool, lost in 1833, and the PICKERING DODGE of Boston, USA, in 1839; all of which lost crewmembers who were buried in the churchyard.

LANCASTER

Type: Sailing Ship, Full Rigged
Port of Registry: Liverpool
Official Number: 101
Tonnage: 353 tons
Built: 1823, Lancaster
Date of Sinking: March 14th 1835
Location: Sarn Badrig, Cardigan Bay

Captain Lethbridge was getting impatient. Although he was in command of a ship he knew well and on a voyage to Africa, a route he was well acquainted with, he was not pleased lying windbound for five days in St Tudwall's roadstead. With a change in the weather on March 14th 1835, the LANCASTER weighed anchor at 11am and proceeded on her voyage; Captain Lethbridge felt much better.

The LANCASTER was owned by Sir John Tobin of Liverpool and the ship made regular trips to Africa. As usual, it was a mixed cargo with puncheons of rum, hogsheads of tobacco and loaves of bread, palm oil, barrel staves, casks of gunpowder and cases of muskets.

Captain Lethbridge may have been overconfident in his pilotage of Cardigan Bay for within three hours of weighing anchor his ship had hit the western end of the causeway known as Sarn Badrig. It was generally thought that Captain Lethbridge had mistaken the position of the causeway.

The Lloyds agent at Pwllheli on hearing of the plight of the ship tried to get a boat out to help but being low water all the vessels were grounded. By the time a rescue boat had reached the LANCASTER she had already broken up and the crew had abandoned the ship.

Large quantities of her wreckage came ashore near Barmouth and the Cambrian newspaper reported that 'most of the articles are in a damaged state, particularly the bread, hats and tobacco-leaf. We regret to find that some of the country people seemed much inclined to plunder the property thus cast upon the shore, and to rapaciously exercise the disgraceful practice of wrecking. They broke open the rum puncheons, and drank to such an excess, that one man died in consequence. A great part of the property would no doubt have been pilfered, had it not been for the strenuous exertions of several respectable inhabitants'.

This is one of many wrecks that is still awaiting discovery by divers in the shallow waters of Sarn Badrig, known in English as St Patrick's Causeway, an area that has seen the loss of countless sailing vessels especially in the eighteenth and early nineteenth century.

LANGTON GRANGE

Type: Cargo Steamer
Port of Registry: London
Official Number: 105831
Tonnage: 5,852 tons register
Built: 1896 Belfast
Length: 420 feet
Breadth: 54 feet
Engines: 568 nhp
Date of Sinking: August 5th 1909
Location: Bell Rock, North Bishops,
Pembrokeshire, Dyfed

A Lloyds Telegram from St David's broke the news that a large ship was on the rocks off the West Wales coast. The telegram read; 'Large four masted steamer ashore on submerged rock, North Bishops - dense fog. Lifeboat alongside, further details will be sent on return of Lifeboat'.

The year was 1909 and a thick summer fog enveloped the sea. The ship was the LANGTON GRANGE steaming south from the Clyde on her way to Newport, Gwent in ballast. She hit Bell Rock, a submerged rock pinnacle that lies a short distance away from the North Bishop. On impact the huge ship slid on top of the reef and remained perched there. Signal rockets were fired from the ship and these were heard on the mainland resulting in the St David's Lifeboat being launched. When they left St Justinian's, the Lifeboatmen did not know where the ship was lying, they had to search in the fog. Eventually they succeeded in discovering her and went alongside. The LANGTON GRANGE was perched at an awkward angle and the Lifeboat stood by for three hours until Captain Groves told the Lifeboat Coxswain that his crew would remain on board as there were other ships in the vicinity.

The LANGTON GRANGE remained in a precarious position and the next day her four hundred and twenty foot long hull started to break apart in the middle. Because of the dangerous condition, the Captain and crew were taken off and taken to Fishguard by tug. They returned the following day but finding the amidships was bulging and the stern settling down in the water, they collected their valuables and left. Five of the LANGTON GRANGE'S boats were towed into Porthclais.

Emblem on the dinner-ware of the LANGTON GRANGE.

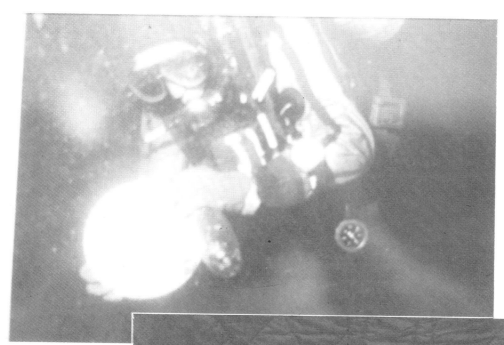

A Swansea diver finds a dinner plate and a tonic water bottle on the wreck at 35m depth.

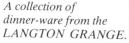

A collection of dinner-ware from the LANGTON GRANGE.

The LANGTON GRANGE was not so lucky and sank on Bell Rock providing divers today with interest at depth. Great care and sea experience is called for in diving in this location as strong currents abound and there are depths in excess of 55 metres to the south of the wreck.

A team of Swansea divers located the LANGTON GRANGE'S wine and champagne storeroom a few years ago and a variety of bottles, still full and corked, have been recovered.

Six days after the stranding of the LANGTON GRANGE, a similarly large steamer the MANATON, also went aground on the north-east ledge of the Smalls Rock. The steamer was almost up to the door of the lighthouse and the 48 men on board could easily have walked off had it been necessary. A salvage vessel working on the LANGTON GRANGE hurried over to help the MANATON, bringing with her some powerful pumps. At the next high tide the MANATON was refloated but not without extensive damage and she was towed to Cardiff for bottom repairs.

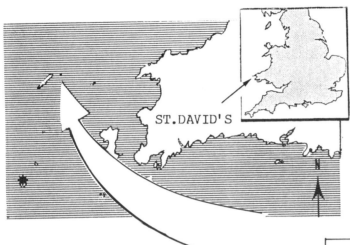

ST.DAVID'S

Bell Rock can only be located successfully by using a depth sounder. Guideline transits, the right hand side of Whitesands in line with Careg Trai. South Bishop Lighthouse between Careg Rhoson and Maen Rhoson.

Not a dive for the inexperienced, dangerous currents likely to take divers off the rock and down to depths of over 50 metres, especially on North-going current. Slack water about 3 hours after Low and High Water, Milford Haven.

Anchor will usually snag into wreckage but may be difficult to retrieve. Currents can be so strong that a small boat may be dragged underwater if anchored on a short warp.

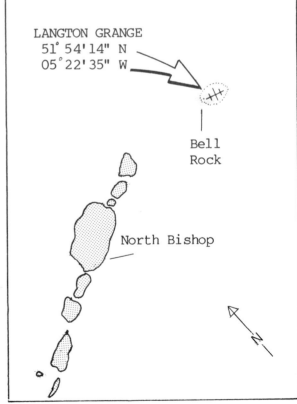

LANGTON GRANGE
51° 54'14" N
05°22'35" W

Bell Rock

North Bishop

DIVE DETAILS
Location: 51°54'14" N 05°22'35" W
Depth: 20m to 40m
Seabed: rock & silt
Currents: dangerous
Underwater Visibility: good
Launch Site: Whitesands or Porthclais

SS LANGTON GRANGE, the large London steamer that became wrecked on Bell Rock in a dense August fog in 1909.

LA PLATA

Type: Sailing Ship, Barque Rigged
Port of Registry: Liverpool
Tonnage: 275 tons register
Date of Sinking: January 1863
Location: Off Point Lynas, Ynys Mon

It was a dark January night in 1863 when an outward bound sailing ship collided with a steamship off the coast of Ynys Mon. So devastating was the blow that despite the fact that both vessels were strongly built of iron, they both sank.

The London and Liverpool steamer LIVERPOOL, owned by Messrs T A Tamplin & Company, had left London on December 30th. On her way to Liverpool she had called at Plymouth and Penzance and was now rounding north Wales on the final part of the journey. On board were 23 crew and 3 passengers. The steamer's course was south east by east when a light was sighted directly ahead. The light was estimated to be about half a mile ahead so their course was altered to south east. After about four minutes it was altered hard over to south south east. The approaching vessel was the barque LA PLATA, starting her voyage from Liverpool to Lima, Peru.

A fresh breeze was blowing from the north east and although the men aboard the sailing ship had seen the steamer's light, they had assumed at first that it was a fixed light on the Skerries rocks.

Twelve minutes later they realized their error but when they saw the starboard light of the steamer they assumed she was safely passed them. The Chief Officer was on watch on LA PLATA and he starboarded the helm when he saw the steamer's green light, it was a costly

LIVERPOOL

Type: Steamer, Brigantine Rigged
Port of Registry: Liverpool
Tonnage: 480 tons register
Date of Sinking: January 1863
Location: Off Point Lynas, Ynys Mon

mistake. All three lights immediately showed from the steamer and he realized they were on a collision couse. He desperately threw the ship's wheel hard aport but the inevitable happened...the barque hit the steamer in the main chains.

The steamer at this moment was already going astern, her Captain explained, 'We had stopped her way, and the engines were reversing when the barque struck us on the port midships with great force. Finding we were fast sinking we got the boats out, and had the passengers and crew safely put into them. Soon afterwards she went down. We were picked up by a schooner and landed next morning at Holyhead'.

The barque had her fore compartment stove-in and she immediately started filling with water. The crew endeavoured to keep her afloat, pumping all through the night. By morning they realized their task was in vain and were forced to abandon her. They took to the ship's boats and were picked up by a passing steamer. LA PLATA sank to the seabed at 10am that morning. It was amazing that there was no loss of life with such a forceful collision and with the sinking of both vessels.

As far as the author is aware the remains of these two ships have not been found or identified. The steamer LIVERPOOL may be easier to locate and identify; as a rough guide she sank between one mile and one and a half miles north north west of Point Lynas.

The sailing barque LA PLATA collides with SS LIVERPOOL off Point Lynas in 1861. Collision was the cause of many shipwrecks around Wales, especially at night or in fog. In this incident both vessels sank but, fortunately, no lives were lost.

LOCH SHIEL

Type: Sailing Ship, Full Rigged
Port of Registry: Glasgow
Tonnage: 1,218 tons
Built: 1877, Glasgow
Length: 225 feet
Breadth: 36 feet
Date of Sinking: January 30th 1894
Location: Thorn Island, Milford Haven,
            Dyfed

The wrecking of the LOCH SHIEL ended up as a 'whisky galore' bonanza for the local people, but started as a brilliant rescue by the Angle Lifeboat.

The LOCH SHIEL was outward bound from her home port of Glasgow to Adelaide, Australia, when bad weather forced her into Milford Haven. She was commanded by Captain Thomas Davies who made a

navigational error and thought he had passed Thorn Island which she struck, head-on. The full rigged ship was badly holed, water flooded-in and she sank down by the stern.

A paraffin soaked mattress was burnt to attract attention and the Angle Lifeboat set out at 10.45pm. The twelve-oared Lifeboat took 6 men from the mizzen rigging and then approached the lee of the island to help the rest

of the crew and passengers who had escaped from the wreck via her bowsprit. The 27 people who had got onto the island were in a spot inaccessible to the Lifeboat and 3 lifeboatmen had to land to help them. In the darkness, it was a difficult task to guide each one of them around the cliffs to the waiting Lifeboat. The rescue took all night and by dawn the 26 crewmen and all 7 passengers had landed safely at Angle.

Customs men discovered hoards everywhere; amongst holes in the cliff, in the roofs of the houses and behind recesses that had been wallpapered over. One hideout was so well concealed that two bottles were found sixty years later when a cottage was being improved.

The RNLI recognised the extremely difficult rescue and three silver medals were awarded.

The LOCH SHIEL was full of the finest Scottish whisky, 'over 7,000 cases of it and a like number of bottled beer and extensive quantities of spirits of every description', if the local press had it right. The beach was completely covered with wreckage, and thousands of bottles of whisky were said to have washed ashore. Such a welcome bonanza

Bricks manufactured near Glasgow, part of the LOCH SHIEL cargo.

had never before arrived on the doorstep of the Angle villagers. For some it proved too much. A father and son were drowned whilst they were towing a keg ashore and another man died from 'excessive whisky drinking'.

The Pembrokeshire Herald four months later commented, 'For a day or two the horses and carts were employed in taking away the spirits and beer wholesale and depositing the different loads in well devised places for the purpose,

A rare photograph taken in 1894. The wreck of the LOCH SHIEL can just be made out to the left of Thorn Island. Her bows point towards the island and 3 masts are still standing.

and subsequently the inhabitants divided the liquor and concealed it in fields, gardens and secret recesses at their homes, of the 7,000 cases of spirits only 2,000 odd have as yet been recovered'.

Customs men discovered hoards everywhere; amongst holes in the cliff, in the roofs of the houses and behind recesses that had been wallpapered over.

One hideout was so well concealed that two bottles were found sixty years later when a cottage was being improved.

A contemporary report said 'the inhabitants paraded the place incapably drunk'. Full bottles are still found today by divers but their contents are unlikely to have the same affect.

Bottle recovered from the wreck

DIVE DETAILS
Location: 51°41'47" N 05°07'07" W
Depth: 10m to 15m
Seabed: rock, kelp & sand
Currents: OK but boat cover required.
Underwater Visiblity: average
Launch Site: Dale, Gelliswick or
            West Angle

Note, intending divers are requested to contact Mr Pearson of Thorn Is, Tel: 064684-225 and Milford Haven Port Authority Tel: 06462-2342, before diving this wreck.

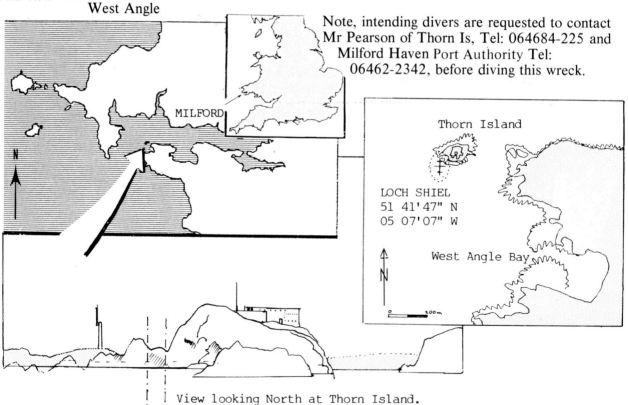

MILFORD

Thorn Island

LOCH SHIEL
51 41'47" N
05 07'07" W

West Angle Bay

0   200m

View looking North at Thorn Island.
Prominent navigation beacon can be seen above the rocks
to the left. Wreck 25 metres out from the island.

LUCY

Type: Coaster
Port of Registry: Delfzijl, Holland
Official Number: 640201
Tonnage: 450
Built: 1964, Westerbroek
Length: 168 feet
Breadth: 28 feet
Engines: Oil, 360 bhp
Date of Sinking: February 14th 1967
Location: Skomer Is., Pembrokeshire, Dyfed.

It was Valentines Day in 1967 when the Dutch coaster LUCY was on her way to Barry from Norway; in her hold was a cargo of calcium carbide. While negotiating the tricky waters of Jack Sound, the coaster suddenly came to a dramatic halt. She had hit one of the submerged reefs and impaled herself on the top of Cable Rock in the middle of Jack Sound.

Flags 'N' and 'C', as international signals of distress, were promptly raised as the skipper, Jan Spaltman, decided on the best action to take. The coaster refused to move from the rock despite the ferocious currents that were sweeping past them. It was decided to leave the ship as it was too risky to stay on board for fear of an explosion if the sea water reacted with the cargo to produce acetylene gas. The 7 man crew and the ship's mascot, a collie dog, abandoned the vessel within half an hour and got clear in the liferaft.

They were later picked up safely and taken to a hotel in Johnston where they spent the night.

The LUCY struck the rock about midday which was a few hours before low water. She remained intact on the rock throughout the afternoon. Just after 6pm with a rising tide and a south east wind force 5-6 she drifted free with a severe list to starboard and part of her decks awash.

The north going current silently took the LUCY into St Brides Bay where she was lost from sight in the gathering gloom. A snowstorm was just starting and her whereabouts were a mystery to all except a local diver who patiently watched all night and was rewarded with seeing her sink 'like the Titanic' on the north side of Skomer Island. The LUCY sank to the dark seabed thirty five metres below and now provides interest to hundreds of divers who visit her each year.

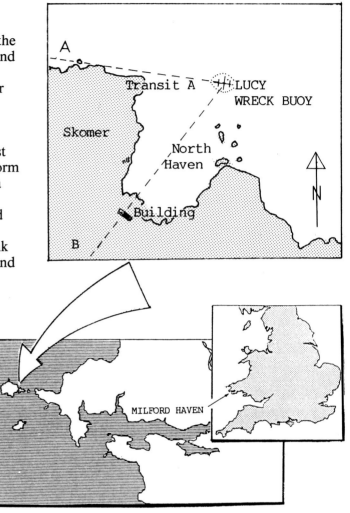

DIVE DETAILS
Location: 51°44'27" N 05°16'33" W
Depth: 33m to 38m
Seabed: sand, silt & gravel
Currents: 1 knot
Underwater Visibility: fair
Launch Site: Martin's Haven

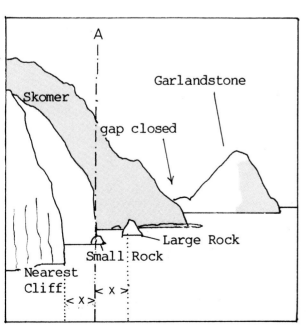

One of the few relatively intact wrecks known to divers in Wales. Lies east/west with bow pointing to Martin's Haven. Wreck usually marked and can tie up to the buoy positioned outside North Haven. Always attempt to surface immediately above the wreck (preferably at the stern) to avoid being run down by the Skomer trip boat which frequently passes close by.

View looking West (280°C) towards Garlandstone. Look for the large rock and the edge of the nearest headland. Transit line is when the second headland bisects and is in line with the small rock.

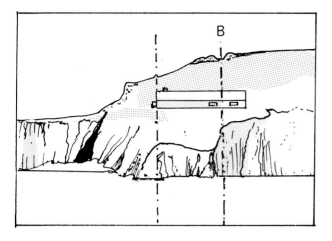

Looking South West (225°C) at the
bungalow above North Haven beach.
Front elevation only, no gable ends
showing. Dip in rocks directly
above division between the last two
windows. Tiny pimple above garage.

Skomer Marine Reserve Management
Committee advise divers to visit
the Information Centre at Martin's
Haven prior to diving this wreck.
Useful information is obtainable
at the centre, including Dive
Guides and Tidetables.

MERKUR

Type: Cargo Steamship
Port of Registry: Finland
Tonnage: 2,593 tons
Date of Sinking: May 9th 1920
Location: Off Barry, Glamorgan,
          Bristol Channel

ZELO

Type: Cargo Steamship
Port of Registry: Newcastle-on-Tyne
Official Number: 140701
Tonnage: 2,339 tons gross
Built: 1917, Sunderland
Length: 285 feet
Breadth: 41 feet
Engines: 3 Cylinder, 249 nhp
Date of Sinking: September 19th 1920
Location: Off Barry, Glamorgan,
          Bristol Channel

Two seperate collisions in 1920 resulted in two cargo steamers sinking in Barry Roads. In May 1920 the Finnish steamer MERKUR was leaving the port of Barry with coal for Las Palmas when she was in collision with another steamer inward bound. She collided with the CASTRO ALEN, a Spanish steamer that was entering for Newport with a cargo of iron ore from Bilbao. The Spanish steamer's bow was severely damaged but she managed to reach Newport Docks. The MERKUR began to sink at once and her crew, including two women were rescued by another steamer and transferred to Cardiff.

The MERKUR foundered in a position near to the Breaksea Light Vessel and a wreck buoy was soon placed to mark the hazard. Salvage operations were carried out during the summer and there were hopes of raising her in the September but the operations were hampered by thick fog.

On the evening of September 19th the ZELO, taking 3000 ton of Bilbao iron ore to Cardiff, arrived on the scene. Darkness had already fallen by the time the ZELO had reached the Nash, and when in Barry Roads she struck the sunken wreckage of the MERKUR.

The ZELO smashed into the fo'csle of the MERKUR and started to sink in a matter of seconds. The entire crew was summoned to the boats, which they hastily did without panic. There were 27 on board including the Captain's wife who was walking on deck when the ship hit. When the alarm went to abandon, one of the the firemen in the engine room immediately stopped the engines and made a hurried escape for the decks, climbing up through a ventilator and injuring his head in the process. A raft was launched and the officers and crew managed to get clear just in time. They saw their ship go down minutes later.

Hearing the shouts for help the steam pilot cutter FANCY went to their assistance, picked up 26 officers and crew up and landed them at the Pier Head. On landing the survivors realized one of their crew was missing. It was the Steward and it was assumed that he was below decks making out the list of goods to be surrendered to the Customs and had become trapped when the ZELO sank.

The South Wales Daily News reported, 'The MERKUR into which the ZELO ran, was sunk in May last in collision, and all through the summer salvage operations have been carried on, but without success. It is now expected that she will have to be blown up.'

MOLESEY

Type: Cargo Steamer
Port of Registry: London
Official Number: 112405
Previous Name: ROKEBY
Tonnage: 3,809 tons gross
Built: 1899, Stockton-on-Tees
Length: 348 feet
Breadth: 49 feet
Engines: 340 nhp
Date of Sinking: November 25th 1929
Location: Midland Isle, Pembrokeshire, Dyfed

The wreck of the MOLESEY in 1929 made world news. She was a thirty year old cargo steamship, originally named ROKEBY, that was hit by a severe gale off the Pembrokeshire coast. The MOLESEY was in ballast from Manchester to Cardiff when she took water into her No.3 hold. Her Captain wisely made for the shelter of Milford Haven when a mechanical failure, some say the steering gear, others say a broken propeller, left her at the mercy of a very severe storm. The ship was taken north into Jack Sound where she smashed against the rocks of Midland Isle. An SOS was sent out from the ship and the Angle Lifeboat went out to help. The Lifeboat failed to find the wreck and

returned empty handed. She later did another trip with the same negative result.

Broadcasting history was made that night when the BBC sent out an SOS asking any ship in the vicinity to make visual or radio contact with the MOLESEY which was being pounded by the waves. The position of the wreck was virtually hidden from the sea but could be seen easily by those on the mainland cliffs. Unfortunately for those aboard the half sunken steamer a breeches buoy was not feasible across Jack Sound.

After seeing a rocket fired from the ship the St David's Lifeboat was launched but when they

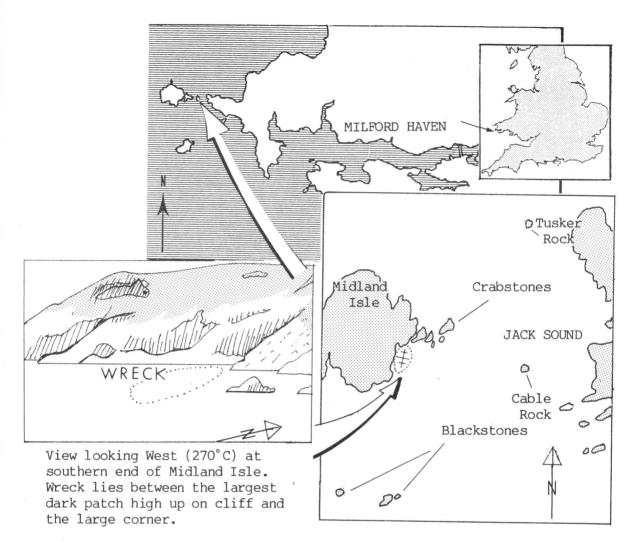

View looking West (270°C) at southern end of Midland Isle. Wreck lies between the largest dark patch high up on cliff and the large corner.

got to the wreck they saw no sign of life and decided to return in the daylight. The plight of those on the MOLESEY was critical. The ship was awash, two of the ship's lifeboats had been smashed and the waves had devastated the bridge. With the Lifeboats failing to get alongside the wreck and a landward rescue impossible those on the MOLESEY were forced to survive as best they could. Most of the crew huddled desperately inside one of the uppermost cabins, some of them spending the night with water up to their chests and praying that the the ship would sink no further. During the night 6 men were swept to their deaths and the wife of the Chief Officer was also lost.

The Angle Lifeboat got to the wreck soon after daylight and took 28 people off, which included 2 foreign stowaways and Sam Brown who was experiencing his seventh shipwreck!

A small Marloes boat was passing the wreck a short time afterwards and sighted another survivor waving frantically from the island near the wreck. He was a Maltese fireman who had hidden himself during the ordeal and surfaced after the rescue. Thinking he was the only survivor he had swum to the rocks wearing a lifejacket. He was landed at Martin's Haven and taken to meet his fellow crewmen at Milford Haven's Sailors' Rest.

DIVE DETAILS
Location: 51°44'02" N 05°15'39" W
Depth: 3m to 7m
Seabed: rock & kelp
Currents: dangerous away from cliff
Underwater Visibility: good
Launch Site: Martin's Haven or Dale

NORMAN COURT

Type: Sailing ship, Barque Rigged
Port of Registry: Greenock
Official Number: 60998
Tonnage: 855 tons gross
Built: 1869, Glasgow
Length: 197 feet
Breadth: 33 feet
Date of Sinking: March 29th 1883
Location: Cymyran Beach, Ynys Mon

A heavy south south west gale was raging when reports reached the Lifeboat Stations that a barque was ashore on Cymyran Beach. The Rhosneigr Lifeboat, THOMAS LINGHAM, went out but the huge breakers smashed into her causing all sorts of problems. Several rowing crutches were broken and one Lifeboatman was washed overboard but saved by his lifeline. The Lifeboat was forced to return home.

The Holyhead Lifeboat was then launched and with the help of a tow from a steamer and a steam tug got to within one mile of the wreck. Under oars, the Lifeboat made three attempts to get through the surf to the men hanging onto the rigging. These attempts failed and five rockets fired from the shore also failed. The Coxswain of the Holyhead Lifeboat considered beaching his boat but decided that it was too risky and so headed for home. The local Rhosneigr Lifeboat once again set forth but had to return. The crew of the NORMAN COURT had spent a whole night and a day hanging on to the rigging and two of them had already died of hypothermia.

Every rescue attempt had been unsuccessful and yet there were still men to be saved. All were wondering what next could be done. When the Holyhead crew heard that the Rhosneigr Lifeboatmen had returned empty handed and utterly exhausted, they decided that there was still time to perform a rescue. The London and North-Western Railway Company provided a special train to convey them to Rhosneigr. On arrival, the Holyhead crew

manned the Rhosneigr Lifeboat and proceeded out to the wreck. In mountainous seas they gradually pulled closer and threw a line to the men. The shipwrecked men lowered themselves one by one into the Lifeboat and 20 were saved.

The NORMAN COURT was built of teak on iron frames secured by brass through bolts stamped with the name of the builder, Inglis.

Painting of the NORMAN COURT under full sail. (See book cover picture for the rescue.)

The Lifeboat Coxswain Thomas Roberts was awarded an RNLI silver medal.

Launched in 1869 as a clipper, the NORMAN COURT was built of both iron and wood in a composite construction. During the peak of the China trade the NORMAN COURT had raced other famous tea clipper ships such as the CUTTY SARK, THERMOPYLAE and TAEPING. It was claimed that she could sail a few degrees closer to the wind than these ships and the NORMAN COURT won the 1872 tea race in 96 days. In 1878 she was rerigged as a barque. On her final voyage she had a cargo of sugar from Java to Greenock and was under the new command of Captain McBride who was subsequently found to have made errors in his navigation.

DIVE DETAILS

Location: 53°14'18" N 04°32'27" W
Depth: 8m to 12m
Seabed: sand
Currents: manageable
Underwater Visibility: average
Launch Site: Rhosneigr

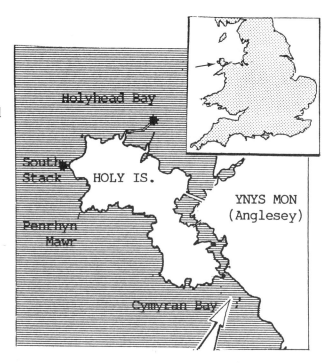

The wreck is on a line between Rhoscolyn Beacon and the southern end of the airfield buildings. The outer rocks of the Cymyran reef are also in transit on this line (transit A). The tower near Silver Bay is in line with the most seaward buildings at Rhosneigr.

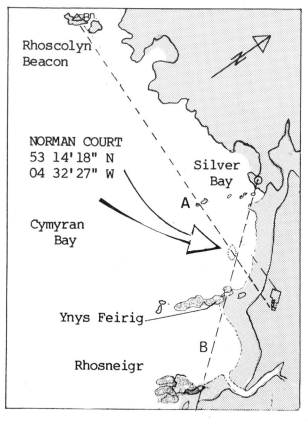

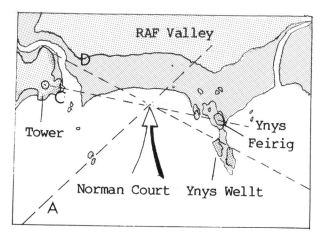

The highest part of Ynys Feirig in line with the Tower (transit C). The landward edge of Ynys Wellt in line with the furthest rocks to the right of the Tower (transit D).

OLINE

Type: Sailing Vessel, Schooner Rigged
Port of Registry: Copenhagen
Date of Sinking: March 23rd 1882
Location: Cat Rock, Newport,
               Pembrokeshire, Dyfed

The schooner OLINE was caught on a lee shore in tempestuous weather in March 1882. She was on a journey to Glasgow with a crew of 5 when she got into trouble a few miles seaward of Cardigan. The sea was one mass of foam and in the late afternoon the schooner could be seen flying signals of distress as she tried desperately to stay out to sea. She was caught in a dreaded north west storm with nowhere to go for shelter and it was an awful dilemma for her Master, Captain Holm, who did not know the coast.

The Coxswain of the Cardigan Lifeboat was called to launch the Lifeboat and he was told that the crew were already waiting at the Lifeboat house. He set off for the Lifeboat Station a few miles away and when he arrived he found few of the crew there and realized that he should have collected them before setting out. Some naval reserves offered their services to act as Lifeboat crew but the Coxswain refused to launch in the terrific seas without the regular crew. As a result the Lifeboat was not launched, a decision which became most unpopular with the local people.

The Newport Rescue Team also saw the OLINE in distress and fired blue rockets in response to flares seen on board the schooner. These were also seen at Fishguard and their No.1 Lifeboat (there being two Lifeboats stationed at Fishguard at that time) immediately launched to help.

Cat Rock, where the schooner OLINE was lost with her crew in 1882.

The Newport Life Saving Apparatus, unfortunately it failed to save the crew.

It was a wild night and the Lifeboat crew had to row for three hours before they could clear Dinas Head, by which time they could no longer see any lights from the schooner. It took them another hour of rowing before they could land at Cwm yr Eglwys. By now it was 4am and the OLINE had been driven ashore on the rocks near Newport.

The Fishguard Lifeboat crew, although cold, wet and fatigued, launched again to the rescue. They got half way to the wreck when a breaking wave hit the Lifeboat and sent two Lifeboatmen over the side. It was pandamonium... the wave had smashed the steering oar and washed away three pulling oars. The men were hauled back and the Lifeboat was forced to return to Cwm yr Eglwys.

The Newport Rescue Team tried everything to help as the schooner came ashore.
The first rocket fired made contact but the OLINE'S crew could not fix the line because of the huge surf sweeping the decks. The

stricken men climbed the mast and hoped for another line to find its target. Unfortunately this did not happen and at 8am the mast fell carrying with it all 5 men who drowned in the surf beneath the cliffs. Scores of Newport people watched, helpless, knowing that no ordinary boat could survive in the conditions. Those that saw the men perish vowed that Newport would have its own Lifeboat Station so that this would not happen again. In less than two years there was a new Lifeboat Station built nearby.

Great criticism was hurled at the Lifeboat crew in Cardigan for not launching their boat, and the Second Coxswain was fired for not complying with RNLI instructions. Those that knew the sea conditions, realized that they were so atrocious that the Lifeboat may not have survived.

The Fishguard Lifeboatmen experienced one of their most heroic service launches, yet, because no lives were saved, it does not even get a mention on the service plaque.

OWEN MORRIS

Type: Sailing Vessel, 3 Masted Schooner
Port of Registry: Caernarfon
Official Number: 92201
Tonnage: 168 tons
Built: 1891, Porthmadoc
Length: 102 feet
Breadth: 24 feet
Date of Sinking: November 1907
Location: Black Rock, Porthmadoc,
Gwynedd

The schooner **OWEN MORRIS** was within hours of completing a lengthy voyage.
She had crossed the Atlantic from Labrador to Italy with a cargo of salted fish and was now returning to her home port of Porthmadoc. Captain David Roberts and the five man crew were looking forward to being home where they could enjoy Christmas with their wives and children.

Within an hour a sudden and unexpected squall entered Cardigan Bay which quickly developed into a full gale. In Criccieth, those that had attended the Sunday morning service were making their way back home. Amongst them were some of the Lifeboatmen who could see the schooner in the bay and suspected that there might be a Lifeboat call-out before the end of the day.

During the early afternoon the OWEN MORRIS was in trouble and Captain Roberts ordered the distress flags to be hoisted. The men and women of Criccieth all rushed down to the beach to watch or participate in the launch of their Lifeboat CAROLINE. Once launched the Lifeboat crew rowed smartly out through the surf line before hoisting the heavily reefed mainsail. After gaining searoom the Lifeboat bore down on the schooner which was dragging across the bay on her last remaining anchor.

The OWEN MORRIS was in a terrible state, her sails in shreds and with one anchor already parted, the men on board could only wait for a

The OWEN MORRIS breaks up at Black Rock.

rescue. The 6 crewmen were greatly relieved to see the rescuers. At the first run-in, 3 men managed to jump into the Lifeboat and the remainder leapt aboard when the Lifeboat came alongside for the second time. With all the schooner's crew safely aboard the Lifeboat returned to Criccieth.

The OWEN MORRIS became entombed in a cave of Black Rock and as the waves rocked the wreck it caused the ship's bell to ring out a haunting note. It was a sad end for a fine schooner that had crossed the Atlantic a score of times.

PAUL

Type: Sailing Ship, 4 Masted Schooner
Port of Registry: Hamburg, Germany
Tonnage: 1,538 tons gross
Built: 1919, Seattle, USA
Length: 230 feet
Breadth: 45 feet
Date of Sinking: October 30th 1925
Location: Towyn Point, Carmarthen Bay,
      Dyfed

The PAUL was carrying a cargo of timber from Halifax, Nova Scotia when she met with gales in the Atlantic. Storms caused her to lose most of her canvas and then fog caused her to lose her way.

She was intending to get to Milford Haven for orders but she went off course and ran onto the sands in Carmarthen Bay. Her crew consisted mostly of Germans, and 11 of the crew of 16 took to the ship's lifeboat. The Ferryside Lifeboat RICHARD ASHLEY was quickly on the scene and picked up the 11 crew, and then returned to the ship to take off the remaining crew and the Captain. The weather was not kind to the tugs that attempted to tow the PAUL off. The Cardiff tug BEAVER made various attempts to get the vessel off but they were unsuccessful and the PAUL ended up firmly stuck in the sand.

Local labour was employed in salvaging the 1,300 tons of Canadian timber which was then sold and put to good use in making roof timbers. The hulk of the PAUL was to become a prominent landmark on the Gwendraeth estuary and for some years her four masts remained standing.

One aspiring salvager tried to raise the hulk on a high tide by putting a large quantity of empty barrels inside the hull. When the tide came in, instead of lifting the vessel, the casks burst through the decks and floated away.

The substantial hull timbers of the PAUL still stick up through the sand to remind us of one of the many sailing vessels to be swallowed up in Carmarthen Bay.

Salvage work commences in 1925.

Five years later her 4 masts were still standing.

PAUL timbers today.

PILOT CUTTER No.5

Type: Sailing Vessel, Cutter Rigged
Port of Registry: Bristol
Tonnage: about 14 tons
Date of Sinking: January 18th 1881
Location: Off Lavernock,
             Bristol Channel

The 1880's saw a considerable number of shipping losses around the coast of Wales. The peak of annual shipwreck losses around the coast of Britain was in 1876 when some 838 shipwrecks were recorded.

A gale which affected the South Wales coast more than any other area happened on January 18th 1881. Hurricane force winds coupled with thick snow and high tides caused a night of terror near Cardiff. It was bad enough for those on land with two houses at Penarth having their roofs completely ripped off and metre deep snowdrifts around Cardiff that stopped the trains. It was the worst snowstorm for forty years but for those at sea it was much worse. Because of the easterly gales there was only a small fleet of ships in the Cardiff roadstead but as the wind increased the vessels at anchor began to drift.

The only place for them to sail was to the flats between Penarth and Lavernock.
This they did and by morning there were seventeen vessels ashore near Lavernock, although most got off without damage.
Amongst them were, the Liverpool ship ETTA, the London iron barque MIRELLA, the ALEXANDRA of St Malo, the WAVE of Gloucester, the ELIZABETH of Waterford, and the ketch RESTLESS of Salcombe. The large vessel BUCKHURST of London, about to depart from Penarth with coal for Bombay parted from her anchors and drove ashore on Penarth beach, colliding with a schooner and a brig on the way.

On the West Cardiff Bank there were six vessels made total losses amongst them the PILOT CUTTER No.5 and the ketch AMAZON of Jersey; the schooner ST ANNE was wrecked near Penarth Head.

On January 17th, Captain Journeay left his ship, the WILLIAM of Yarmouth, Nova Scotia, at anchor in Penarth Roads. He had a shock when he returned some hours later to find his ship had vanished.

Failing to find her, all he could do was start an embarrassed wait hoping it would be found as he was on a voyage from Sharpness to Boston, USA. The WILLIAM had slipped her anchors and run out to sea but the Liverpool tug FIERY CROSS found her, and although dismasted by the gale, she was successfully docked at Cardiff on the 20th.

Two barques were also driven from their anchors near Cardiff to land on the Somerset coast. The 337 ton TARSUS of Littlehampton struck the rocks near Minehead and the Norwegian barque AMERICA came adrift at Penarth to land near Warren Point.

A hand bellows foghorn as used on trading schooners, fishing sloops and pilot boats throughout the nineteenth century.

The easterly wind was so cold that it caused the river at Monmouth to freeze over for more than a mile. Navigation at sea became guesswork, for visibility was reduced to a few metres in the blinding snowstorm. The PILOT CUTTER No.5 was doing her best to help the vessels stranded on the West Cardiff flats when she was run down by another vessel. The Pilot vessel quickly sank and the crew had a lucky escape but had no time to recover any of their clothes or belongings. It was a sad loss especially as the same vessel had been in an incident two months before when 2 men had lost their lives. Both men were from Pill, the small village on the banks of the River Avon and the heart of the Bristol Pilot community.

RENE

Type: Sailing Ship, Barque Rigged
Port of Registry: Nantes, Brittany
Tonnage: 383 tons gross
Built: 1867, Nantes
Length: 119 feet
Breadth: 27 feet
Date of Sinking: January 8th 1886
Location: Overton Cliffs, Gower,
    Glamorgan

Villagers in Overton suspected that the strong gale of the previous night might have caused a shipwreck on the cliffs of the Gower. Their suspicions were increased when, in the early hours of the morning, a strange wet black retriever dog was seen wandering about in a forlorn state. A farm worker then discovered a group of men in a bedraggled condition walking over the cliff path. They were wet, bruised and badly injured and were the only survivors of a barque that had smashed itself to pieces at Kilboidy during the night.

The entire story then emerged. The Breton barque RENE was outward bound from Cardiff with 450 tons of coal for Arcachon, near Bordeaux. She had left Cardiff early, two days before, and had reached Nash Point where they met a calm. She anchored for six hours while the tide was against them and then proceeded with a fresh south west wind.

The wind increased to gale force and with driving sleet the Captain had difficulty in navigating. After leaving the Mumbles light the men were ordered aloft to take-in canvas as the vessel was speeding along too fast. With two almighty shudders the ship's hull hit the shallows of the Helwick sand bank. The sails were backed to try and get her off the sandbank and the barque immediately responded but sailed straight for the Overton cliffs. She hit at about low water and the full force of the sea drove incessantly into the wreck.

The men wanted to lower the lifeboats to abandon the ship but Captain Gouzer told them that they would not survive in the surf and advised against it. Shortly afterwards the main and mizzen masts crashed down smashing both ship's boats.

The Captain then decided that their only chance was to try to swim for the shore. He took off most of his clothes and told his crew 'look after yourselves and do the best you can', he then plunged overboard and was never seen alive again.

A cabin boy and a seaman followed the Captain but the remainder of the crew sensibly waited on the ship until the planks broke apart beneath their feet. The water was terribly cold and at 4.30am there was only a small piece of wreckage left and all the men had been washed off by the waves. 6 men survived in the water and clambered ashore, severely injured but alive. They wandered about until daybreak having lost three of their comrades, their Captain, and all of their possessions.

John Bevan looked after the men at his farmhouse and gave them food and medical attention. The Porteynon Lifeboat was about to be launched when they received a message that all was lost as the ship was already a total wreck.

A bedraggled dog was the first indication of a nearby shipwreck.

ROTHESAY CASTLE

Type: Early Paddle Steamer
Port of Registry: Liverpool
Tonnage: about 200 tons
Built: 1816, Dumbarton
Length: 93 feet
Breadth: 16 feet
Engines: Twin-cylinder Compound, 34nhp
Date of Sinking: August 18th 1831
Location: Dutchman Bank, Conway Bay,
　　　　　Gwynedd

The ROTHESAY CASTLE was one of the first commercial steamers to be built. She was designed for the relatively quiet waters of the River Clyde and was built in 1816 at Dumbarton.

Some fifteen years later she was so worn out, leaky and rotten that some of her crew refused to sail on her. It was in this deplorable condition that her owners, the Liverpool and Beaumaris Packet Company, decided to cash-in

The ship's funnel toppled and waves swept over the deck washing passengers into the sea.

on taking holiday sightseeing trips from the busy quayside of Liverpool to the seaside port of Beaumaris.

The air was festive and everyone was in a holiday mood as the small steamer left George's Pierhead. The ship's band was playing a happy tune as they proceeded out of the Mersey. The passengers were not to know it was a day trip to disaster.

As they neared Beaumaris the steamer met with worsening weather and gradually one by one everyone became sick and frightened. The Captain was an ex Naval man and had been drinking heavily since leaving the quayside. When the passengers implored him to return he shouted that there would be little profit in it and totally ignored their pleas. The steamer was two hours late in departing partly due to a London gentleman wanting to take his horse carriage with him. The delay meant that the steamer had a rougher passage and a longer one and eventually reached a position five miles from Beaumaris at about midnight.

The rough seas had opened up the seams and water was rushing into the cabins and into the engine room. The paddles stopped working when water flooded over the fire box. Quickly the steamer was driven onto the nearby shallows of Dutchman Bank and was soon breaking apart. On board were 165 people who were now in great danger.

The ROTHESAY CASTLE carried no distress flares, no signal guns nor signal lights and was unable to show her distess in the darkness. Her equipment was useless; she only

The pilot ingeniously escaped.

had one ship's lifeboat and that was damaged and lacked oars and was originally designed for 18 persons.

The ship's funnel crashed first crushing the steward and his wife and toppling onto passengers on the starboard side. Waves swept over the wreck sweeping people into the water at each stroke.

By daylight there were only 23 survivors. Some saved themselves on a makeshift raft using the large skirts of one of the passengers as a sail. Another survivor was a local Pilot who had the foresight to take both buoyancy and sail with him when he was being washed overboard. Grabbing hold of a barrel and taking with him a parasol he managed to sail to safety.

Criticism was thrown at the owners for allowing such an unsound vessel to go to sea and also that the ROTHESAY CASTLE was improperly manned and her Captain and Mate drunk. The incident brought about the establishment of the Penmon Lifeboat station in 1832 and the Penmon Lighthouse in 1837.

ROYAL CHARTER

Type: Sailing Clipper with Engine.
Port of Registry: Liverpool
Tonnage: 2,719 tons register
Built: 1855, Flintshire
Length: 336 feet
Engine: Auxillary, 200hp
Date of Sinking: October 26th 1859
Location: Moelfre, Ynys Mon

Luxuriously appointed, the ROYAL CHARTER was a fast iron clipper, built in 1855 specially for the Australian run. Between her three tall masts she had a funnel serving a 200 hp engine, designed to maintain her overall speed when in light airs. Her owners, the Liverpool and Australian Steam Navigation Company were proud to say that they could transport passengers to Australia within two months of leaving Liverpool.

On her last voyage the ROYAL CHARTER was returning to Liverpool. She had left Melbourne on August 26th 1859 and was entering Liverpool Bay after a fast 15,000 mile crossing of both the Pacific and the Atlantic. It was inconceivable that such a large ship, well accustomed to the rigours of Cape Horn, could be wrecked within hours of her home port.

The ROYAL CHARTER under sail.

While rounding the Skerries the gale increased to east north east force 10. When seven miles off Port Lynas, signal rockets and blue lights were fired to attract the attention of a Pilot. Although Pilot Boat No.11 saw the lights, he was also battling in the seas and could not help.

Within half an hour the wind strength had increased to hurricane force. The two bladed propeller and the small engine could do nothing to help the clipper in the ebb tide and with one hundred mile per hour winds the ship could make no headway. The difficulty Captain Taylor had was that there was no sea room to sail into Liverpool Bay and try as he might the ship refused to answer the helm; the ship continued to drift towards the shore.

An hour before midnight they anchored four miles out but the fury of the storm broke the cables and she headed for the rocks. She drove ashore, bows on, only ten metres from the land. Joe Rodgers, a Maltese seaman, jumped into the water and swam a line ashore to the villagers who promptly rigged up a bosun's chair. The women passengers were offered the lifesaving chair but refused because they were either too modest or too frightened to use it. Valuable time was wasted as the immense seas showed no mercy and waves, reported as being eighteen metres high, were smashing into the hull every few seconds.

The greatest tragedy was now to happen. Suddenly the ROYAL CHARTER'S hull broke apart washing hundreds of men, women and children into the sea. Others jumped overboard thinking they could merely wade ashore but instead sank into six metres of breaking foam. Passengers with sovereigns in their pockets and gold miners with their hard earned wealth in their money belts unsuccessfully tried to swim ashore. One man, who failed to make it, was found with £320 worth of gold on him that had dragged him to his death. No women or children were saved and only 39 men survived.

The ROYAL CHARTER was indeed a treasure ship, for she had £322,440 of gold coins in her strong-room, in addition, many of her passengers were carrying undisclosed amounts of money and gold.

Divers were soon employed to work on the wreck during the winter of 1859 and it was reported that all but £30,000 was recovered. Some further £1,200 was handed over to the Receiver of Wreck, but the whereabouts of the rest will never be known.

There are undoubtedly many small personal objects and odd gold sovereigns still to be found amongst the shallow water but, like all such wrecks, it is probably uneconomic to spend the time and effort in their search.

Contemporary etching from the Illustrated London News showing ROYAL CHARTER breaking up on the rocks.

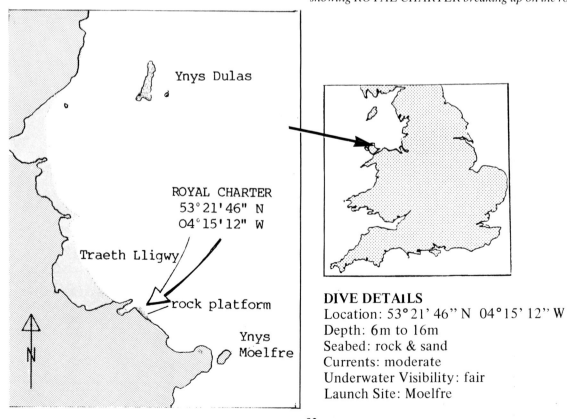

Ynys Dulas

ROYAL CHARTER
53° 21' 46" N
04° 15' 12" W

Traeth Lligwy

rock platform

Ynys Moelfre

N

DIVE DETAILS
Location: 53° 21' 46" N 04° 15' 12" W
Depth: 6m to 16m
Seabed: rock & sand
Currents: moderate
Underwater Visibility: fair
Launch Site: Moelfre

SALUS

Type: Sailing Ship, 3 Masted Barquentine
Port of Registry: Shoreham
Official Number: 58026
Tonnage: 264 tons register
Built: 1863, Southwick, Sussex
Date of Sinking: September 25th 1896
Location: Strumble Head, Pembrokeshire, Dyfed

A force 9 gale from the north north east caused seas of tremendous proportions outside Fishguard. It was 1.40pm on September 25th 1896 and a rougher sea had not been seen for many a long year. Despite the conditions a three masted barquentine was seen standing out to sea instead of running directly for Goodwick beach which a Captain with local knowledge would have done. Although many on shore thought she was in trouble, no distress signals were being shown.

The vessel was obviously trying to continue her journey southwards and attempting to round Strumble Head, but the weather proved too much for them. An hour later the barquentine was in trouble, her lower fore-topsail torn in shreds and she had no headsails up. Distress signals were immediately hoisted; the ensign at half-mast with the union jack upside down.

The Coastguards immediately fired a rocket to muster the rescue company, there being insufficient time to perform a Lifeboat rescue. One of the Coastguards kept a constant lookout on the distressed ship through a telescope and could see 7 men in the rigging clinging desperately to the ropes and another man at the ship's wheel. Then suddenly a huge sea swept clean over the ship and it was some time before she righted herself. The man at the helm was then seen to join his crew in the rigging. The ship was less than a mile from the shore and within twenty minutes she struck the rocks.

The cliff rescue team hurried towards Strumble Head but by the time they arrived the ship had already smashed herself to bits and they could find no survivors.

Port lights, hull pins and a rudder plate from the SALUS.

The Pembrokeshire Herald reported, 'within four minutes of the time when she struck, all was hopelessly lost. The poor fellows on board had not a vestige of a chance of life, seeing that a high precipice towered above them against which the waves dashed with immeasurable force. The vessel's timbers were torn asunder, and before anyone was able to approach with assistance, if assistance was possible, which is very doubtful, the heart rending calamity was complete. There was nothing in sight, with the exception of small bits of wreckage, the largest piece recovered being a spar about fifteen feet long'.

The SALUS was owned by Richard Keason, of King's Hill, Arklow; this also being the Master's name. Coastguards picked up the bodies of two seamen both of which were

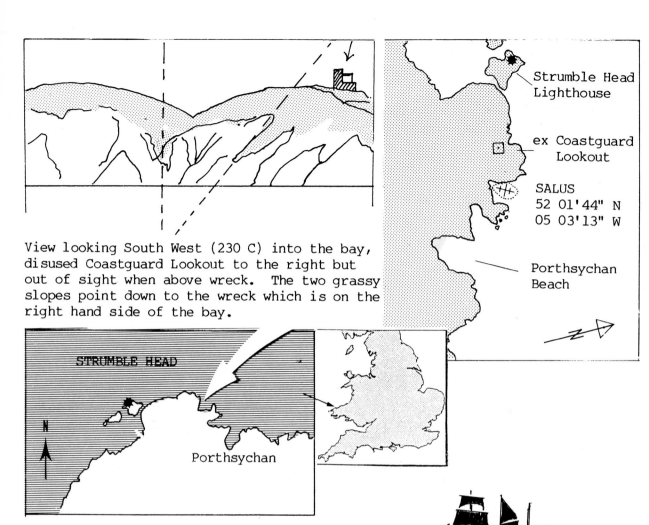

View looking South West (230 C) into the bay, disused Coastguard Lookout to the right but out of sight when above wreck. The two grassy slopes point down to the wreck which is on the right hand side of the bay.

identified by the tattoos they bore on their forearms. Also to come ashore were woollen drawers, presumably of the Captain as they had the initials R.K. on them. It was feared that a woman had been lost as a white hat also washed ashore.

The last whole remnant of the SALUS to be picked up was the figurehead of a woman typically painted green by its Irish owner.

DIVE DETAILS
Location: 52°01'44" N 05°03'13" W
Depth: 4m to 11m
Seabed: rock, kelp & boulders
Currents: none (close in)
Underwater Visibility: good
Launch Site: Goodwick
Comments: Sheltered in SW winds but a long sea trip from any launch site (6 miles)
Anchor chain strewn along west side of the bay, parts of davits to be seen inside the cave. Small bits of iron frames scattered over the seabed.

SAMTAMPA

Type: Cargo Steamship
Port of Registry: London
Official Number: 169787
Previous Name: PALEG WADSWORTH
Tonnage: 7,219 tons gross
Built: 1943, Portland, USA
Length: 423 feet
Breadth: 57 feet
Date of Sinking: April 23rd 1947
Location: Sker Rocks, Glamorgan

The most terrible shipwreck tragedy within living memory to happen along the South Wales coast occured in 1947. It was a double catastophe as it resulted in the loss of a large ship with the whole of her crew and also the loss of the Mumbles Lifeboatmen who went out to save them.

Bow section of the SAMTAMPA. This photograph was taken in 1947 on the saddest of mornings when it was realized that 39 had been lost from this ship and a further 8 Lifeboatmen, the entire Mumbles crew, who went to their assistance were also drowned.

The SAMTAMPA, a large cargo ship, formerly a Liberty Ship, was on a voyage from Middlesbrough to Newport, in ballast.

A strong westerly gale was in progress when she entered the Bristol Channel and the ship developed an engine fault. Prudently her master, Captain H.Neale Sherwell, decided to drop anchor in Swansea Bay so that the trouble could be sorted out. The weather in the bay was getting worse by the minute. At 4.38pm the starboard anchor chain parted and twelve minutes later the port cable snapped. The huge, relatively light hull, was taken eastwards in the hurricane force winds. Within twenty minutes the SAMTAMPA was on the rocky ledges near Sker Point.

The Mumbles Lifeboat EDWARD, PRINCE OF WALES was launched just after 6pm to go to the rescue. William Gammon, who had been Lifeboat Coxswain for seven years, was at the helm of the lifeboat as they headed out across the bay. At the same time the Porthcawl Coastguards and rocket team were attempting to get a line to the wreck from the shore. The wind was said to be in excess of one hundred miles per hour and, in less than five minutes of the SAMTAMPA hitting the rocks, she was starting to break up.

Two hours later she was a total wreck, the terrifying ten metre waves having broken her into large pieces. The rocket apparatus was ineffective in the tremendous winds and it failed to get a line out to the wreck. In fact some of the rockets were driven back so far by the wind that they landed in the fields behind the operators. Not one of the 39 crew on board the SAMTAMPA was saved, and by morning the full disaster was realized.

The Lifeboatmen had failed to return and the Lifeboat was found smashed and upside down on the rocks further along the beach. All 8 Lifeboatmen had been lost. When news reached Mumbles the whole town was in mourning.

The people of Porthcawl still remember that night and the ship's lights remained brightly lit on the bridge and engine room section although the SAMTAMPA had broken into three parts, making the whole scene a horrifying spectacle.

A new Lifeboat came to the Mumbles that July, and there were many men eager to join the crew; as a mark of respect to a heroic Coxswain the Lifeboat was named WILLIAM GAMMON.

EDWARD, PRINCE OF WALES
Mumbles Lifeboat donated by the Welsh
    Lifeboat Fund

Type: RNLI Motor Watson Lifeboat
Official Number: RNLI 678
Tonnage: 16 tons
Built: 1924, Cowes
Length: 45 feet
Breadth: 12 feet
Date of Sinking: April 23rd 1947
                    On Service
Location: Sker Rocks, Glamorgan

This Lifeboat's usual crew was 8 men, the number that was tragically lost on her final rescue attempt. During her lifetime at Mumbles from 1924 to 1947 she saved no less than 129 lives.

SHEPTON MALLET

Type: Sailing Ship, (Square Rigged)
Port of Registry: Bristol
Tonnage: assumed about 180 tons
Date of Sinking: February 12th 1731
Location: Pilton, near Worm's Head,
         Gower, Glamorgan

The square-rigged vessel SHEPTON MALLET was returning home to Bristol with a valuable cargo from the West Indies when she hit the Gower coast.

She was nearing the end of a long voyage, with a cargo of cotton and sugar from Barbados packed tightly over a cargo of ivory tusks taken on board on the Ivory Coast as a form of stabilising cargo.

She hit the Gower cliffs of Pilton in February 1731, and the contents of her cargo were quickly dicovered and were plundered by the local people. Customs officers had the difficult task of combing that area of the Gower to locate the whereabouts of the missing property.

The 'much plundered' cargo comprised 72 hogsheads of sugar, 19 tierces (a tierce is a cask of 192 litres or 42 gallons), I bagge of cotton and 204 elephants' teeth.

Notices were posted by the Customs throughout the Gower warning that if the missing property was not brought 'forthwith the goods to ye Customs House, Wharehouse or Mr Caleb Thomas's at Pitten, they will be prosecuted as the law directs'.

This must have helped in securing some of the cargo. The Customs men managed to do a reasonable job as, three days later, it was reported that they had seized some of the ivory; '51 of ye teeth are saved and secured under the King's lock'.

The master of the SHEPTON MALLET was William Hellier and he, together with 5 of his crew, survived the shipwreck.

STUART

Type: Sailing Ship, Barque Rigged
Port of Registry: Liverpool
Official Number: 76549
Tonnage: 912 tons
Built: 1877, Dundee
Length: 203 feet
Breadth: 34 feet
Date of Sinking: April 8th 1901
Location: Near Porthcolman, Lleyn,
Gwynedd

On April 5th 1901, STUART, a Liverpool barque, was being towed out of the Mersey by a tug. Her crew were starting what they thought was a long voyage to New Zealand and none of them realized that he would get no further than the North Wales coast.

When they cast off from the tow the wind was south and they set off on a long port tack towards the Irish coast. There she tacked against the headwind and hoped that the starboard tack would take her clear of Bardsey Lighthouse. This was not to be and the thick drizzle that prevailed obscured their sighting of the Caernarfon Bay Lightship which would have confirmed their position.

The STUART'S speed was greater than expected and before avoiding action could be taken she ran headlong onto the shore. She hit the rocky coast eleven miles north of Bardsey in the early hours of Easter Sunday morning.

The crew immediately abandoned the ship taking to the lifeboats and spent the next few hours looking for a landing place when in fact they only needed to wait for low water and wade ashore.

Amongst the considerable cargo was a large number of whisky cases destined for New Zealand and Australia. Stories of local people hurrying to the scene to 'rescue' the valuable liquid were commonplace. Even an entire Sunday school and its teacher joined in to help!

The Liverpool Salvage Association immediately sent an Assessor to the site who reported; 'The STUART lying one quarter of a mile west of Porth Colmon, on rock, heading NE, broadside to sea, and listed seaward 8 degrees. Depth of water alongside ten feet aft, with water rising and falling in the hold with the tide. Ground very uneven, large boulder evidently through the bottom between mainmast and after hatch. Sure to break up first strong wind from westward'.

He recommended sending a small steamer to save some of the stores and cargo. This was duly done and the large iron hull of the STUART gradually broke apart.

There are still pieces of iron plates marking the spot where the STUART met her final resting place, but most of the pieces are amongst the kelp in two metres depth of water.

Photograph on the opposite page shows the STUART breaking apart on the rocky beach near Porth Colman in 1901. Debris from the barque litters foreground. The size of the vessel can be appreciated by comparison with the people walking amongst the rocks. With magnifying glass have a look at the group of figures immediately below the centre broken hull, is that the Sunday School teacher and her pupils?

THETIS

Type: Submarine, Triton Class
Port of Registry: British, Royal Navy
Tonnage: 1,095 tons
Built: 1939, Cammell Laird's, Liverpool
Length: about 240 feet
Date of Sinking: June 2nd 1939
Location: 25 miles off Point Lynas,
        Ynys Mon

The submarine THETIS was undergoing acceptance trials in Liverpool Bay when disaster struck. She failed to surface after diving and 99 lives were lost.

There were 103 persons on board when the first and fatal dive was made in the waters about thirteen miles north of Llandudno. As soon as the dive had commenced (June 1st 1.50pm) those in command knew that all was not well. The submarine was too light on the surface and descended slower than expected. The indicators showed that all the bow caps were closed but in fact one of them had been left in the open position flooding torpedo tube number five. When the Torpedo Officer went to check, he found the test cock had been painted over and he opened the chamber door

HMS THETIS outside the yard where she was built in 1939. She was to sink twice in the next four years, and 161 men were to lose their lives.

with drastic consequences. Water poured into the two forward compartments and the submarine plummetted and lurched and settled nose down on the seabed with her stern bobbing above the waves.

The impact, when she hit the seabed forty metres below, destroyed the wireless and signalling equipment. They could not contact the surface vessels and could only release the forward indicator buoy which was not seen until that evening. It was 7.30am the next morning (fifteen hours later) when the stern of the THETIS was located.

Signals were made by tapping through the hull and everyone inside the submarine was still alive, but without lights and surviving at an angle of 42 degrees to the horizontal.

Strong tides prevented the stern of the THETIS being lifted out of the water and when a hawser broke, contact was lost.

Those on the surface were expecting the men to escape from the Davis Escape Hatch but only 4 men escaped successfully. Those that tried to follow had problems and further

Her stern could not be lifted and she sank to the seabed.

attempts were not made. None of the other 99 men was seen alive again.

The THETIS was salvaged from the seabed using slings and a tidal lift, four metres at a time, and beached at Lligwy Bay near Moelfre. The submarine was refitted at the Birkenhead yard and a year later was relaunched under the new name of THUNDERBOLT. She was lost after being depth-charged with all her crew off Sicily on March 13th 1943 and a further 62 men lost their lives.

TRELAWNY

Type: Sailing Ship, Full Rigged
Port of Registry: Bristol
Tonnage: 295/320/333 tons
Built: 1781, Bristol
Date of Sinking: December 11th 1806
Location: Nash Point, Glamorgan

Outward bound for Jamaica, the full rigged ship TRELAWNY met with disaster soon after leaving her home port of Bristol.

In 1806, Bristol was one of the largest ports in the world. It was a usual sight, each December, to see over thirty West Indiamen set sail heavily laden bound for sunny Jamaica. The cargoes were varied, including all manner of goods useful to the settlers in the West Indies. It was in the days when ships were constructed heavily of oak and had hull shapes unsuitable to the task of sailing out of the Bristol Channel against the prevailing south westerly winds.

The TRELAWNY struck the platform of rocks beneath Nash Point in the early dark hours of December 11th 1806. Her weary twenty five year old hull quickly smashed to pieces. In a desperate struggle the men tried to launch one of ship's boats and at the same time the mainmast crashed down onto the deck, killing the Captain. The ship broke apart in the surf throwing everyone, including passengers, into the water.

When the final tally was made it was found that 12 people including the Captain had been lost. Some of the crew and the Bristol Pilot managed to escape in one of the ship's lifeboats.

A contemporary account gave the following information, '17 persons were taken off pieces of the hull of the TRELAWNY, a West Indiaman, which here went to pieces'.

VAINQUEUR

Type: Sailing Ship, unknown rig
Port of Registry: Dieppe, France
Owner: Harve de Grace
Date of Sinking: December 17th 1753
Location: Sker rocks, Porthcawl,
            Glamorgan

Fruit intended for the winter banquettes of French nobility ended up in Welsh cottages surrounding Margam and Pyle, just before Christmas 1753.

LE VAINQUEUR, a French vessel belonging to Harve de Grace was returning home from Lisbon. Her Master, Captain John Masson had made the mistake of entering the Bristol Channel instead of the English Channel; an error which was common before and since. His ship became stranded at 'a place called ye Scar'. She became completely wrecked and was extensively looted by crowds of people.

Captain Masson's mistake was caused by poor weather, but it cost him his life and his ship. The cargo list of the ship was an interesting one; 789 chests of China oranges, 650 frails (rush baskets) of figs, 240 boxes of lemons and 84 planks of Brazilian hardwood.

When the ship struck, it started to break up quickly. Captain Masson, his brother, who was the Mate, and a passenger were all drowned. 8 of the crew, however, were saved. An eye-witness account said that when he went to look at the wreck on Sker Rocks he saw a crowd of 400 people swarming all over the vessel trying to get at the cargo, rigging, iron and broken planking. The wreckers robbed the dead body of the Captain, removing 17 gold Portuguese coins, 3 French crowns, his silver watch (which was later recovered) and the silver buckles from his shoes and breeches. It was also said that the wreckers tried to set fire to the hull so that the iron could be recovered.

Such practice was not uncommon, especially as many of the people regarded a wrecked ship as a divine gift and some fervently believed that ships wrecked on those rocks were the right of the local populous.

The authorities were shocked at the wrecking and one of the enforcing officers stated that if they had known sooner they could have caught 'the villains'. This, however, may not have been the case because another report said that when a bailiff went to recover some of the cargo an angry mob threatened him with his life. He promptly left the scene and said he would not return even if he was offered £50.

Lloyds List summed up the event by saying 'the Country people made a perfect wreck of the Ship and Cargo'.

Shipwrecks since 1830

How many shipwrecks are there around the Welsh coast? This is a question that I continually get asked, so I thought it was time I looked for an answer.

If Wales is divided into North and South with Aberystwyth as the dividing line but also including in South Wales some of the losses in the northern part of the Bristol Channel and some of the Severn Estuary, then 44% of wrecks happen in North Wales and 56% in South Wales.

Based mainly on Board of Trade figures, I calculate the following;

1830 to 1850 - 2,020 wrecks
1851 to 1880 - 5,040
1881 to 1930 - 4,700
1931 to 1981 - 2,500
                ——————
Total   14,260

As can be seen the greatest number of losses were in the latter half of the nineteenth century. To give an example; in 1868 there were 202 shipwrecks around the coast of Wales as compared with only 94 in 1908.

As sport divers are well aware there is only a small percentage of these wrecks that are likely to be of significant interest to them. Some shipwrecks have been smashed so completely that nothing is left or lie undiscovered under tons of sand, or are at depths beyond that likely to be reached by amateurs. If we say a mere 3% are of interest to the diver then it still means that there are over 400 diving interest wrecks around the Welsh coast. Out of these divers presently know the locations of about one third of them.

Bibliography

BENNETT,T.H. Welsh Shipwrecks,1,11,and 111,(Haverfordwest,1983)
BOSWELL,D. Loss List of Grimsby Vessels 1800-1960,(Grimsby Public Library,1969)
British Vessels Lost at Sea, 1939-1945 (Patrick Stephens,1976)
EDMUNDS,G. The Gower Coast, (Regional Publications,1979)
EAMES, A. Ships and Seamen of Anglesey,(Anglesey Antiquarian Society,1979)
EVANS,A.L, Some Pirates, Smugglers & Wrecks in the Bristol Channel,(Port Talbot,1984)
FARR,G. Wreck & Rescue in the Bristol Channel 11.(Bradford Barton,Truro,1967)
FARR,G. Shipbuilding in the Port of Bristol,(National Maritime Museum,No.27,1977)
FENTON,R. A Historical Tour Through Pembrokeshire,(1811)
GODDARD,T. Pembrokeshire Shipwrecks,(Hughes,1983)
HOCKING,C.A. A Dictionary of Disasters at Sea in the Age of Steam,1824-1962,1 & 11,(Lloyds Register of Shipping,1969)
JONES,I.W, Shipwrecks of North Wales,(David & Charles,1973)
HOWELLS,R. The Sounds Between,(H.G.Walters,1968)
HOWELLS,R. Across the Sounds to the Pembrokeshire Islands,(Gomer,1972)
LARN,R. Shipwrecks of Great Britain and Ireland,(David & Charles,1981)
LEWIS,E.A. The Welsh Port Books 1550-1603,(1927)
LUBBOCK,B. The Colonial Clippers,(J.Brown & Son,Glasgow,1921)
LUND,P.& LUDLAM,H. The War of the Landing Craft,(Foulsham,1976)
Maritime Wales, Cymru A'r Mor, Nos 1 to 10 (Gwynedd Archive Service,1984)
McALISTER,A.A. H.Hogarth & Sons,(World Ship Society,1976)
McKEE,A. The Golden Wreck,(Souvenir Press,1961)
MORRIS,J. The Story of the Holyhead Lifeboats,(Coventry,1979)
MORRIS,W. Plans of Harbours,etc.,St George's & Bristol Channels,(Shrewsbury,1801).
NICHOLSON,J.A. Pembrey & Burry Port, Their Harbours, Shipwrecks and Looters,(Llanelli Borough Council,1985)
PARRY,H. Wreck & Rescue on the Coast of Wales,1,(Bradford Barton,Truro,1969)
REES,P.H. Gower Shipwrecks,(C.Davies,1978)
ROSCOE,T. Wanderings & Excursions in South Wales,(London,1844)
SKIDMORE,I. Anglesey & Lleyn Shipwrecks,(C.Davies,1979)
SMITH,C. The Men of Mumbles Head, (Gower Press,1977)
ZANELLI,L. Shipwrecks Around Britain,(Kaye & Ward,1970)

Newspapers, Magazines & other references

Board of Trade Annual Returns of Shipping Casualties
BSAC Wreck Registers
Brown's Nautical Almanac 1889, 1908.
Cambrian News, from 1808
Cardiff Times, 1858 to 1928
County Echo, 1893 onwards
Dewisland & Kemes Guardian, 1861 to 1882
Diver magazine, 1980 onwards
Flintshire Herald
Graphic, 1869 to 1901
Haverfordwest & Milford Haven Telegraph, 1854 to 1919
Illustrated London News, 1842 to 1900
Lloyds Manusript Wreck Registers, 1855 to 1895
Lloyds Register of Ships 1764 to 1970
Lloyds List, 1741 to 1826
Nautical Magazine
Pembrokeshire Herald, 1844 to 1924
Red Dragon, 1882 to 1887
Sea Breezes, 1932 onwards
South Wales Press, 1867 to 1934
The Times, 1788 onwards
The Lifeboat, RNLI quarterly.
Welshman, 1829 onwards
Western Daily Press, 1858 onwards
Western Mail & Echo, 1869 onwards
Western Telegraph, 1937 onwards
West Wales Guardian, 1927 onwards

Index

Ships and Lifeboats are in capitals.
For surnames of Captains look
under the heading of Captain.

About the Author

An Environmental Health Officer by profession, Tom Bennett lives in Pembrokeshire, and has been passionately collecting shipwreck details for about seventeen years. He started diving in Wales in 1968 and is a British Sub-Aqua Club Instructor who has visited at least 45 wreck sites around Wales.

When he is not diving or writing shipwreck books (this is his fourth), he sails. He has cruised extensively, sometimes solo, around the coasts of Wales, Isle of Man, Isles of Scilly and the entire eastern coastline of Ireland. He has often crossed the Bristol Channel and St George's Channel and seen at first hand some of their moods.

Royal National **Lifeboat** Institution

The RNLI exists to save lives at sea. Since it was founded in 1824, volunteer Lifeboatmen have saved over 114,000 people. Over 1,000 are now saved every year.

It is a voluntary organisation and funded entirely from voluntary contributions. There are 260 Lifeboats on station and the running costs and provision of new lifeboats adds up to over £26 million each year.

Many of the Lifeboats and much of the equipment has been provided by people who have remembered the RNLI in their will.

If you would like to make a donation or know more about how to remember the RNLI in your will, please contact:

The Director
Royal National Lifeboat Institution
Poole
Dorset BH15 1HZ

or Telephone 0202 671133